PUB WALKS
— NEAR —
Bristol & Bath

Dear Huw,

   Happy Birthday!
May you have many
     sunny, drunken walks!

        lots of love

             camie

Other areas covered in the Pub Walks series include:

Berkshire
Buckinghamshire
Cheshire
The Chilterns
The Cotswolds
Dartmoor and South Devon
Derbyshire
Essex
Herefordshire
Hertfordshire
The Isle of Wight
Lancashire
Leicestershire and Rutland
Lincolnshire
Middlesex and West London
Norfolk
Northamptonshire

Nottinghamshire
North Wales
Oxfordshire
Shropshire
South Wales
Surrey
The Surrey Hills
Suffolk
The Thames Valley
Warwickshire
Wiltshire
Worcestershire
East Yorkshire
North Yorkshire
South Yorkshire
West Yorkshire

*A complete catalogue is available from the publisher at
3 Catherine Road, Newbury, Berkshire.*

PUB WALKS
— NEAR —
Bristol & Bath

THIRTY CIRCULAR WALKS
AROUND INNS NEAR BRISTOL & BATH

Nigel Vile

COUNTRYSIDE BOOKS
NEWBURY, BERKSHIRE

First Published 1994
© Nigel Vile 1994

COUNTRYSIDE BOOKS
3 Catherine Road
Newbury, Berkshire

ISBN 1 85306 274 X

Designed by Mon Mohan
Cover illustration by Colin Doggett
Photographs and maps by the author

Produced through MRM Associates Ltd., Reading
Typeset by Paragon Typesetters, Queensferry, Clwyd
Printed in England

Contents

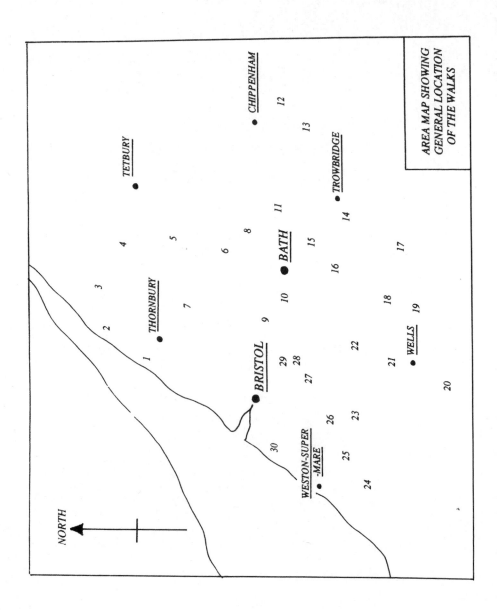

AREA MAP SHOWING
GENERAL LOCATION
OF THE WALKS

NORTH

Publisher's Note

We hope that you obtain considerable enjoyment from this book; great care has been taken in its preparation. However, changes of landlord and actual closures are sadly not uncommon. Likewise, although at the time of publication all routes followed public rights of way or well-established permitted paths, diversion orders can be made and permissions withdrawn.

We cannot accept responsibility for any inaccuracies, but we are anxious that all details covering both pubs and walks are kept up to date, and would therefore welcome information from readers which would be relevant to future editions.

Introduction

The countryside around Bristol and Bath offers a fine natural setting for each of the walks included in this book. This is an area with a tremendously rich and varied landscape. To the west lie the Severn Estuary and the Bristol Channel, a unique environment of mud flats and estuarine wildlife. Northwards are the Cotswold Hills, where numerous stone villages have launched any number of picture postcards and calendars. To the south of Bristol and Bath lie the Mendip Hills, a vast area of limestone upland, dissected and riddled by gorges and pot-holes. Finally, there is the common thread that links these two great cities – the river Avon. The river bank provides some of the most popular walking in the area.

Each walk is centred on one of the many historic inns that grace the area around Bristol and Bath. The aim is to provide as rich a variety of watering holes as possible. This means that, alongside the traditional freehouses and pubs owned by small independent brewers, you will find inns that belong to the nationwide chains. A pen portrait of each pub is provided – its history, its character, the food on offer and the range of beers and ales available. Generally speaking, most pubs should be open at lunchtimes between 11.30 am and 2.30 pm with food being available between 12 noon and 2 pm. Equally, in the evenings you can expect the opening hours to extend from 6 pm until 10.30 pm, with food available from around 7 pm. However, pub opening hours are the subject of constant change and variation, depending upon demand, seasonal factors and occasionally the whim of the landlord. Therefore, rather than specify opening hours in each case, only to be proven wrong by the time the book goes to print, each pub's telephone number is included should you wish to make a precise enquiry. Most pubs display their opening hours at their main entrance, enabling this information to be obtained before you set off on your walk.

The walks are deliberately of modest length, making them suitable for all kinds of walkers from the more mature person to the typical family group. Each should provide a morning or an afternoon of exercise and interest, which can be followed by a relaxing meal and a drink in the relevant pub. Whilst the directions and sketch maps in the book are adequate for route-finding – compasses won't be needed in this part of the world – it is better for the walker to back this up with an OS map. The appropriate OS Landranger sheet, 1:50 000, is specified for each walk, and should be as much a part of your equipment as the obligatory waterproof clothing and stout footwear.

Parking should be done with due consideration. If you intend to visit the pub following the walk, then it is only common courtesy to seek the landlord's permission prior to leaving your vehicle in his empty car park in the morning. On most occasions, landlords are only too happy to oblige. If you are doing a walk and not visiting the pub, then you have no right to use the patrons' car park. Whatever the circumstances, in most cases I have indicated alternative parking arrangements in the vicinity of each pub.

At the end of your walk, you could well be hot and sticky, damp and muddy. It is only polite therefore to both the landlord and his other customers if you attempt some form of wash and brush-up after your walk. If nothing else, at least leave muddy walking boots in your car.

I hope that this book will bring you many hours of pleasure. Not only do these walks open up the countryside around two of Britain's greatest cities, they also introduce some of our finest inns and public houses. I wish you many happy hours of walking.

Nigel A. Vile
spring 1994

① Littleton upon Severn
The White Hart

The White Hart is a lovely old inn, with whitewashed walls and gabled windows. It possesses a traditional and timeless feel, like so many of the other fine examples of English architecture down in the Severn Vale. Stepping inside the White Hart, the visitor experiences a very real feeling of going back into the pages of a history book. Wooden and tiled floors, rugs, wood panelling, exposed beams, a large open fireplace and a wood-burning stove all lend the White Hart a truly rustic atmosphere. This décor is complemented by the pine tables and chairs, the bench seats, the wooden settles and bar stools. Around the walls hang a large number of attractive pictures and prints, including several of life on the nearby estuary, whilst the shelves display pots of flowers, cider jars and various items of china. Hanging from the ceiling are a number of interesting items, including a yoke and bunches of dried hops. It is refreshing to see the family room, as well as the lounge and public bar area, tastefully decorated.

The bar food at the White Hart is generous and imaginative. Starters could include prawn cocktail or garlic mushrooms, whilst the main courses are salads, grills, ploughman's and filled jacket potatoes as well as the house specials. Amongst the dishes that caught my eye were salmon steaks, brewery beef, Malay baked chicken, nut roast and vegetable lasagne. Children are not forgotten, with the ever-popular beefburgers, fish fingers or chicken nuggets served, quite appropriately, with beans and chips. The daily specials are chalked up alongside the bar, and could include, for example, German frankfurter soup, smoked mackerel and cheese quiche, and 'proper' Cornish pasties. Bread and butter pudding, apple pie and sticky toffee pudding are some of the traditional sweets on offer.

The White Hart has been taken over by Smiles, a small Bristol-based brewery. Smiles Bitter, Best Bitter and Exhibition are all available, as well as other excellent West Country brews such as Wadworth 6X and Long Ashton cider. Smiles has an excellent reputation in the Bristol area, and its imprint is stamped all over the White Hart. Tradition, originality and a relaxed air dominate this quite superb inn.

Telephone: 0454 412275.

How to get there: Littleton upon Severn is not the easiest of places to find. The best bet is to follow the A38 northwards out of Bristol as far as Alveston, 12 miles from the city centre. From Alveston, turn on to the B4461 Aust road, and in 3 miles you will find an unclassified road leading into Littleton. The White Hart lies in the centre of the village.

Parking: There is a patrons' car park to the rear of the White Hart. It is perhaps more considerate for walkers to park carefully on the roadside somewhere in this quiet village.

Length of the walk: 5 miles. Map: OS Landranger 172 Bristol and Bath (GR 596901).

A fine excursion that explores part of the atmospheric Severn Estuary between Avonmouth and Gloucester. From Littleton, deep in the Severn Vale, the walk follows the riverside path through to the neighbouring village of Oldbury. The extensive mud flats will provide a focus of attention for ornithologists. In Oldbury, St Arilda's church sits proudly atop an isolated knoll overlooking the mighty Severn. Quiet lanes and field paths lead back to Littleton and the White Hart inn.

The Walk

Walk northwards along the lane outside the White Hart for just a couple of hundred yards to a road junction. Turn left, and follow the cul-de-sac signposted to Whale Wharf, for ¾ mile down to the banks of the Severn. Climb the sea defences and enjoy the panoramic sweep of one of the country's great estuaries. The muddy inlet close at hand is in fact Whale Wharf – over 40,000 visitors flocked here in 1885 to witness the suffering of a stranded whale. Follow the sea defences

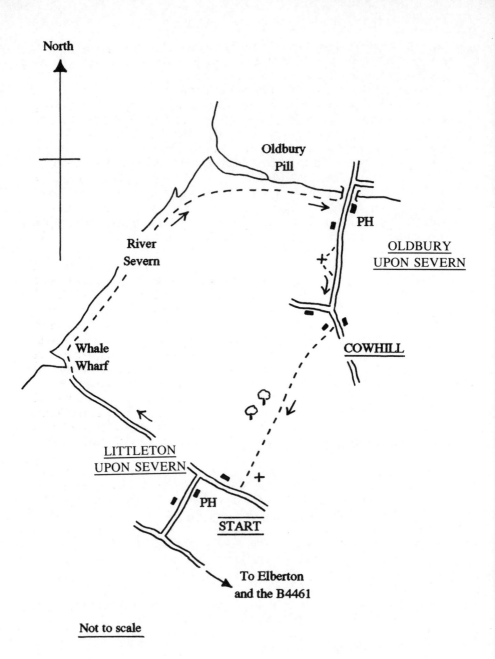

North

Oldbury
Pill

River
Severn

PH

OLDBURY
UPON SEVERN

Whale
Wharf

COWHILL

LITTLETON
UPON SEVERN

PH

START

To Elberton
and the B4461

Not to scale

12

through to Oldbury (away from the Severn Bridge), all the while enjoying the wonderful views across to Wales as well as the bird-life on the nearby mud flats (tides permitting).

As you reach Oldbury, the defences sweep to the right to follow the south bank of Oldbury Pill, an inlet that is the base for the local sailing club. Just before the sluice gate, go down off the bank and head across the fields in the direction of the village. The path crosses a stile into a horse-riding area, before passing among stables to emerge in the village. The Anchor Inn is a few yards down the road to the left.

To return to Littleton, turn right and follow the road uphill past the school and as far as St Arilda's church. It is worth taking a detour to visit the church, which sits proudly atop a small knoll, if only to enjoy the fine views across the Severn from the churchyard seats. If you walk around the church, you will find a gate in the hedge that brings you back on to the Oldbury to Littleton road.

Continue along the lane for 300 yards as far as the hamlet of Cowhill, where one cottager proudly advertises 'Cowhill Cider'. The traditional cider press can be glimpsed in a small outbuilding. When you reach a farm and cottages on your left-hand side, look out for a cottage positioned sideways on to the road on the right. A small footpath sign is attached to the garden gate. Turn right, pass through the garden, and shortly you will emerge into a small orchard (supplier of Cowhill apples for the Cowhill Cider). Bear immediately to the left to reach a stile in the corner of the orchard.

Beyond the stile, you emerge into a large open field. Follow the hedgerow on your left for ¾ mile, through a couple of large fields, until you reach a copse. The path continues alongside this and into a third field. Once again, follow the left-hand hedgerow through to a gate in the corner of the field. This brings you out on to a lane alongside Littleton church. Follow the lane down to a road, turn right and continue past Corston Farm to the road junction encountered at the start of the walk. Turn left, and it is just a few yards back to the White Hart.

2 Shepperdine
The Windbound

The Windbound, on the banks of the Severn Estuary, was actually known as the New Inn for many years. An interesting story lies behind its more recent name. Bargees carrying loads of coal up and down the river would often put in at Shepperdine for a drink-or-seven. This left them in no fit state to continue their journey, so the excuse given to their masters was that they had been 'windbound'. The nickname became so familiar that the pub's name was changed. Drunkards were not the only hazard along the river bank – when excessively high tides forced their way up the river, the sea wall was often breached and it was not unknown for the water to pour down the inn's chimney.

The Windbound sits beneath the sea dyke, with its upper dining-room enjoying extensive views across the river to the Welsh coast. The downstairs bar sits almost below sea-level, whilst picnic tables on the dyke provide a fine vantage point in the summer. The furnishings consist of dining chairs and straight-backed settles that form booths around the pine tables. Local prints and water-colours adorn the walls, together with salmon putchers used to catch fish on the river. In midwinter, with piercing winds blowing up the estuary, the inn's open fire provides welcome warmth.

Bar food includes soup, sandwiches, ploughman's and salads, whilst a daily range of specials is chalked up alongside the bar. Examples are tuna and pasta bake, leek and potato soup, chicken and noodles, Spanish tortilla and sausage casserole. The beers on offer at the Windbound might include excellent brews from Bass and Tetley, as well as Flowers Original. This is a first-rate pub with a real sense of history, enjoying one of the finest locations in the Bristol area.

Telephone: 0454 414343.

How to get there: Follow the A38 northwards out of Bristol for 14 miles until you see 'Oldbury-on-Severn' signposted on the left-hand side. As you approach Oldbury, Shepperdine appears on the signposts. Follow these signs for 'Shepperdine and the River' until you reach the Windbound at the end of a cul-de-sac.

Parking: There is a large car park outside the Windbound, with additional room for careful roadside parking alongside the dyke.

Length of the walk: 7 miles. Map: OS Landranger 162 Gloucester and the Forest of Dean (GR 613961).

The Windbound sits alongside the Severn Estuary, beneath a dyke that protects the inn from the high tides. From the river, this walk heads inland to the village of Hill, where the slightly elevated church and the adjoining Hill Court bring views westward to the river. A bridlepath leads back to the Severn, where the sea defences are followed to return you to the Windbound. Isolated beacons serve as a reminder that this is a navigable stretch of water.

The Walk

Walk back up the lane away from the Windbound for ¾ mile, passing through the scattered hamlet of Shepperdine. Where the road bends to the right, alongside a telephone box, turn left on to a bridlepath. In 50 yards, turn right to follow a second bridlepath shown on the OS sheets as 'Harestreet Lane'. In ¾ mile, this secluded path joins Hill Lane. Turn left and, in less than ¼ mile, a footpath is signposted leading into the field on the right-hand side.

The field paths through to the neighbouring village of Hill are not well defined and the less adventurous may prefer to follow the lanes shown on the map. Intrepid explorers, however, should leave the road and follow the left-hand field boundary through the next couple of fields. Leave the second field through a gateway, and immediately cross a pair of gates on the left-hand side, both of which have clearly seen better days. In the next field, follow the right-hand boundary to

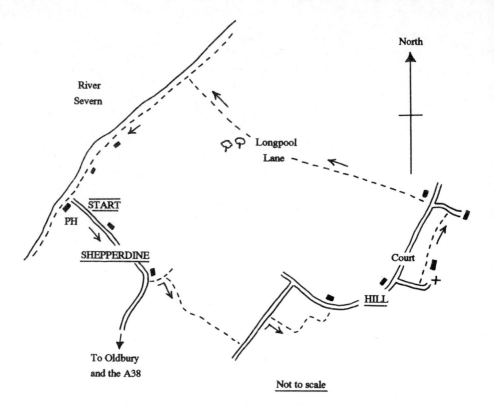

the corner, before crossing another gate on the right-hand side. Follow the field edge to the left, passing a small pond, to another ramshackle gate on the left. Having negotiated this, head straight across the next field to a gateway and the road alongside Scotlands Farm.

Turn right, and follow the lane through the village of Hill. In ¾ mile, turn right on to a driveway signposted as leading to St Michael's church. Just as this lane bears to the left to climb the final few yards to the church, pass through a handgate on the left-hand side to enter the parkland that fronts Hill Court. Go over the first field, passing in front of this 19th century pile. Cross an iron fence at the appropriate point – a somewhat disguised stile – and head directly across the second field to a clearly visible wooden stile. Pass through the gateway at the opposite side of the next field, continue on to a second gateway, and finally aim for a stile that brings you out on to the driveway leading to Upper Hill Farm. Turn left and walk the short distance to the road.

Directly opposite, alongside Brick House Farm, a bridlepath heads down towards the Severn. This path continues for 1½ miles as a lonely, enclosed track. The first section of this path is labelled as 'Stuckmoor Lane' on the 1:25 000 maps, with its final ½ mile shown as 'Longpool Lane' – the adjectives are wholly appropriate! The bridlepath ends at a gateway, beyond which you follow a couple of narrow fields directly ahead for the final ½ mile down to a sluice gate and the banks of the Severn.

Turn left at the river and follow the flood defences back to the Windbound. This stretch is quite superb – wide expansive views, mud flats, wading wildfowl and a pair of beacons to guide ships navigating the Severn. This is a part of the walk where you will undoubtedly pause frequently to breathe in the unique atmosphere. All too soon, the inn comes into sight – and journey's end.

3 Ham
The Salutation Inn

Ham is a small village community straddling the B4509 less than a mile to the south of Berkeley. In the centre of the village sits the Salutation Inn, an unpretentious and charmingly old-fashioned local. It almost gives the impression of being a detached country cottage, with its whitewashed walls, dark paintwork and slate roof, topped-out with a trio of fine chimney pots. To the front of the inn is a pleasant garden with a number of picnic tables, giving views across the Severn Vale towards the Forest of Dean. Restless youngsters will find the play area at the rear of the inn much to their liking.

Internally, the Salutation is divided up into the traditional lounge bar and public bar. These carpeted bar areas are furnished simply, with a small number of tables and chairs, along with cushioned bench seats and bar stools. On the walls and shelves in the bars are displayed a number of horse prints, brasses and cider pots.

Substantial helpings of delicious home-cooked food are served. Choices include ploughman's, chicken Kiev, cheese and broccoli bake, tuna salad, gammon, wings of fire, sandwiches and soup. The egg and bacon sandwich comes highly recommended – thick, crusty bread, fried eggs and whole rashers of bacon. No frills, no nonsense,

simply good honest platefuls of well-prepared food. There are a number of beers and ciders, including Whitbread, Bass, Flowers, Guinness and Dry Blackthorn. This down-to-earth pub offers a friendly welcome to locals and visitors alike.
Telephone: 0453 810284.

How to get there: Follow the A38 northwards from Bristol for 17 miles to the village of Stone, and join the B4509 Berkeley road. Ham is 2 miles from Stone, and the Salutation lies on the right-hand side as you enter.

Parking: There is a car park alongside the Salutation, and room for some roadside parking.

Length of the walk: 6 miles. Map: OS Landranger 162 Gloucester and the Forest of Dean (GR 680983).

Ham lies just outside Berkeley, the Gloucestershire town best known for its castle and the Edward Jenner Museum. From the Salutation, we follow the Little Avon upstream towards the neighbouring village of Stone, before heading cross country to the Whitcliff Deer Park. From here there is a fine walk across the hilltop ridge that dominates the deer park, returning us to Ham and the Salutation. A perfect introduction to the delightful Vale of Berkeley.

The Walk
Follow the B4509 northwards towards Berkeley, passing the hunt kennels and crossing the Little Avon. Just 200 yards beyond the river, turn right on to a footpath signposted to Woodford. Bear half-right across the large open field ahead to reach the river bank.

Follow the bank upstream, ignoring the bridge across the Little Avon, alongside Brownsmill Farm, in a little under ½ mile. Continue along the riverside path for a further mile until you reach Matford Bridge. Cross the river and continue across the field ahead to the corner of the hedgerow some 100 yards away. Keeping the field boundary to your right, walk across the fields until you join the Ham to Stone road in ¼ mile. Turn left for just 150 yards to a road junction, where you bear right onto the Thornbury road. Continue along this quiet lane for ½ mile until, just past some cottages on the left-hand side, a bridlepath crosses the road.

Turn right on to the bridlepath, a secluded green lane. In 400 yards, cross a footbridge on the right into an adjoining field. Turn immediately to the left and cross this field to a stile beneath an isolated tree. Beyond this stile, keep walking in the same direction across the next couple of fields, using stiles to locate the right of way, until you

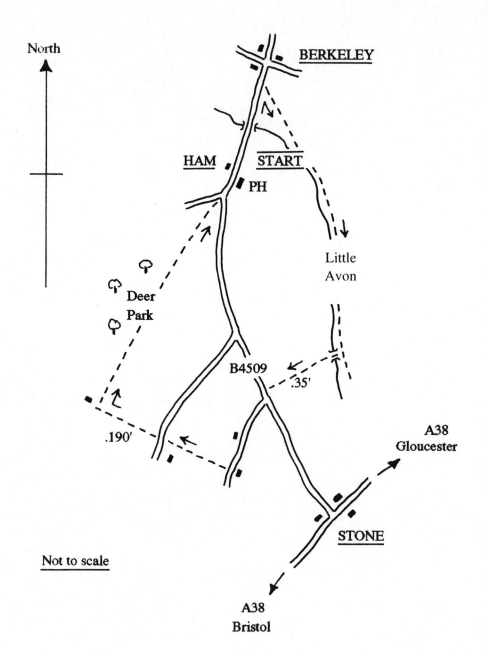

North

BERKELEY

HAM   START

PH

Little
Avon

Deer
Park

B4509

.35'

.190'

A38
Gloucester

STONE

A38
Bristol

Not to scale

join a quiet lane. Almost opposite, the path enters a field and follows the left-hand field boundary, uphill, towards the Whitcliff Deer Park high on the ridge. At the top of the field, cross a stile and turn right to climb to the perimeter wall surrounding the deer park. Follow the end wall of this park until you approach a lodge. Just in front of this lodge, a step stile on the right takes you into the park. Follow the path across the ridge for 1½ miles until it drops downhill to cross a field before reaching the Ham road. Continue the few yards ahead into the village, and the Salutation.

Wotton-under-Edge
The Royal Oak

Wotton is a picturesque town, literally nestling under the Cotswold Edge, as the name suggests. The origins of the settlement date back to medieval times, when Wotton became an important centre for the woollen trade. To this day, sheep and teazels still feature on the town's coat of arms. The Royal Oak is a busy town-centre pub, located almost on the junction of the High Street with Haw Street. Whilst the whitewashed walls could place this hostelry virtually anywhere, the stone-tiled roof will leave you in no doubt that this is a Cotswold pub. Visitors who care to use the inn's secluded rear garden will be able to glimpse the nearby Wotton Hill, from where the Cotswold Way descends steeply into the town.

Internally, the Royal Oak offers public and lounge bars, together with a restaurant area. The bars have been modernised in recent years, and are comfortably furnished with carpeting and reproduction table and chair sets. A selection of rustic prints adorn the walls, including a number of illustrations of ducks and other wildfowl, whilst a high shelf around the lounge/dining area houses a good collection of china plates. A couple of items that caught my eye were a collection of cigar cards featuring transport from years gone by, together with a cricket bat signed by members of the Samuel Whitbread XI. Cricket buffs will read some of the names with a tinge of nostalgia.

An extensive range of traditional bar food is available at the Royal Oak, including omelettes, sandwiches, salads, ploughman's, basket meals and lasagne. There is also a more substantial menu in the restaurant, where hearty appetites can be satisfied with, for example, pan-fried trout or half a crispy duck. Each day, a range of specials is displayed in the bar. These might include steak and kidney pie, game pie, and ham and broccoli flan. As this is a Whitbread house, such brews as Whitbread Best Bitter and West Country Pale Ale are on offer, together with Boddingtons, Bass and Murphy's Stout.

Telephone: 0453 842316.

How to get there: Wotton-under-Edge lies north of Bristol on the B4058 Nailsworth road. As you enter the town centre on the B4058, the Royal Oak is on the left-hand side, in Haw Street, immediately before its junction with the High Street.

Parking: There is a large car park for patrons, behind the Royal Oak. There is also unrestricted roadside parking just along Haw Street from the pub.

Length of the walk: 3 ½ miles. Map: OS Landranger 172 Bristol and Bath (GR 755933).

Driving into Wotton-under-Edge from the south, visitors will immediately be impressed by its location. Wotton sits beneath the steep scarp slopes of the Cotswolds, which rise well over 300 ft above the town. This short circuit encompasses both the historic streets of Wotton's town centre and the hilltops to the north. The views across the Severn Vale to the river and beyond are quite magnificent, so be sure to pick a clear, fine day for this excursion.

The Walk

From the Royal Oak, walk a few yards along Haw Street to Wotton's High Street. Turn right and walk the length of the High Street, a refreshing mixture of small independent shops, including a number of excellent bakeries. At the bottom of the High Street, turn left into Church Street and continue to the main road – the B4058. Cross over, and continue along the B4058, passing the local war memorial and St Mary's church.

Take the second turning on the right past the church – Valley Road – and follow this lane as it bears to the left to pass the backs of several old houses and workshops. At the end of Valley Road, where it bears left to return to the B4058, keep straight ahead, following a tarmac footpath that borders a stream. You are now on a section of the Cotswold Way.

Follow this path on to a lane, where you turn right. Almost immediately, leave the lane and turn left to continue along the Cotswold Way. Initially it is an enclosed path, but it soon crosses a stile to become a field path alongside a delightfully clear stream. All around you are the hillsides and valleys that form the focus of this particular walk.

At the far side of the field, cross a stile to join a lane in a hamlet shown on the OS sheets as Coombe. Turn left for just a short distance, before turning right on to a private road signposted as a footpath leading to Tyley Bottom. About 300 yards along this road, turn left on to the signposted footpath which again points the way to Tyley Bottom. This path climbs to an open field, where you follow the right-hand hedgerow alongside a secluded lake to a second stile in the corner of the field. Beyond this stile, turn left along a bridlepath that very gently begins to climb out of the valley bottom.

The bridlepath joins a lane, where you continue ahead for just a few yards before bearing to the right at a fork. Continue all of the way up this lane for ¼ mile, ignoring any side turnings, as far as its junction with the B4058. This has been quite a climb, but fortunately there is a seat at the road junction – and it enjoys a superb view across the town of Wotton.

Suitably refreshed, cross the main road and follow the footpath opposite signposted to Waterley Bottom. This climbs the hillside very

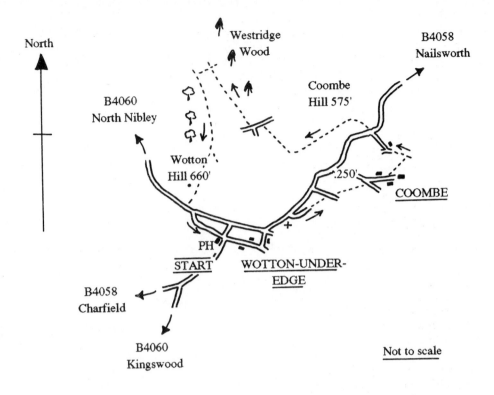

North

Westridge
Wood

B4058
Nailsworth

Coombe
Hill 575'

B4060
North Nibley

Wotton
Hill 660'

.250'

COOMBE

PH

START

WOTTON-UNDER-
EDGE

B4058
Charfield

B4060
Kingswood

Not to scale

steeply for no more than 200 yards to a point where you must look
out for a stile on the left-hand side. Cross this stile, and follow the path
beyond across the hilltop. This path literally clings to the level, right
across the hilltop, and brings with it spectacular views of the Cotswold
Edge and the Severn Vale. (You will not find this path marked on the
Landranger sheets, but it does appear on Pathfinder maps. Purists may
care to note that it runs from 765944 to 761941.)

This superb hilltop path eventually bears sharply to the right to
reach a gate/metal stile. Cross the stile, and follow the footpath
beyond for little more than 300 yards to a small coniferous plantation.
Fork left at this point, to follow the path across the scrubland to join
the Old London Road high on the Cotswold plateau. Turn left along
this road for just a few yards, before turning right onto a bridlepath.
Continue along this bridlepath for ½ mile – it soon borders an
extensive area of coniferous woodland known as Westridge Wood –
until you come to a major junction of paths. Take the very first path
on the left, which borders the edge of an open field.

In 100 yards, this path reaches a cross track. This is in fact the

25

Cotswold Way. Turn left, and follow the main bridlepath for ½ mile as it runs along the edge of the woodland. The Way is shown by blue arrows superimposed with a large white circle. At the end of the woodland, the path forks. The blue arrow – the bridlepath – bears left. Our route follows the route to the right, marked by a yellow arrow, a field path alongside the edge of the trees. In the corner of this field, on your right, cross a stile and follow the path to a clump of coniferous trees.

These trees mark the summit of Wotton Hill. The views from this spot are expansive, and it comes as no surprise to find that at least five seats have been placed on the hilltop for the benefit of visitors and residents of Wotton alike. At your feet lies the town itself. The Cotswold Edge stretches away to the south, whilst to the west lies the Severn Vale, the river Severn and the Forest of Dean. Beyond Wotton Hill, follow the path that drops steeply downhill to join the B4060. Turn left, and follow this busy thoroughfare for 300 yards as far as the first turning on the right. This is Bradley Street, and it passes many attractive cottages before reaching the junction of Haw Street with the High Street, alongside which stands the Royal Oak.

 Hawkesbury Upton
The Fox

Hawkesbury Upton is a hilltop village, located above the Cotswold Edge overlooking the Severn Vale. At one time, a market, serving the local farming community, existed in the village. The Fox was then a gathering place for the local farmers, where each week they would meet to share a communal loaf, cheese and ale. In those days, the village could boast no fewer than seven pubs, a number of which were celebrated in a local rhyme:

'White Horse shall hunt Fox and drink the Beaufort dry,
Turn the Barley Mow upside down and make the Blue Boy cry.'

Today, only the Fox and the Beaufort Inn survive, and the village's farming community has been largely replaced by city commuters. Despite the changes, however, this inn still conveys a good deal of traditional charm.

The Fox is a fine old building, hewn from the local Cotswold stone. Like many inns nowadays, the flower boxes and hanging baskets that adorn the window ledges and walls add a fine splash of colour. Internally, it has been tastefully modernised. There is an abundance of refurbished stonework and beams, together with a large fireplace fitted out with a wood-burning stove. The pictures and prints around the walls are certainly more original than in many pubs. The local sports teams' photographs are proudly displayed above the bar, whilst black and white shots of the village are on view throughout the lounge. An old advertisement for the Stroud Brewery Company catches the eye, as does a historic document informing residents about a property auction in the village.

The inn's menu covers steaks, grills, sandwiches, platters, salads and sweets. Various specials are also displayed on a board in the bar, for example, cold pork, chips and salad, Spanish quiche, and cheese and onion quiche. The sweets on offer at the Fox are particularly appealing and include such delicious options as rhubarb crumble, banana split, lemon lush pie, apple and cherry pie, fruits of the forest cheesecake and profiteroles. The beers on offer include Flowers, Boddingtons and Smiles.

Telephone: 0454 238219.

How to get there: Hawkesbury Upton lies 1 mile west of the A46 Bath to Stroud road, 4 miles north of Old Sodbury. From Old Sodbury, head northwards until you reach the Petty France Hotel at Dunkirk. Shortly after the hotel, a left turn is signposted to Hawkesbury Upton, and the Fox is on the right-hand side as you enter the village.

Parking: There is a car park for patrons in front of the Fox, as well as ample roadside parking in the vicinity of the inn.

Length of the walk: 5½ miles. Map: OS Landranger 172 Bristol and Bath (GR 780869).

Hawkesbury Upton lies high on the Cotswold plateau. It is a large village best known for the Somerset Monument, a superb vantage point across the Severn Vale. From the village, we follow quiet lanes below the hills through to Hawkesbury and Horton. Hawkesbury possesses a church the structure of which is out of all proportion to the size of the local population, whilst Horton Court is one of the area's finest National Trust properties. The return to Hawkesbury Upton follows a section of the Cotswold Way. From this long-distance footpath, fine views extend across the Severn Vale towards the Forest of Dean and the Welsh Hills.

The Walk

From the Fox, continue westwards through Hawkesbury Upton village. On the edge of the village, you will pass a rather attractive group of farm buildings, on the left-hand side, that front on to a quaint pond. The Hawkesbury Monument, a daunting 145 step climb to its

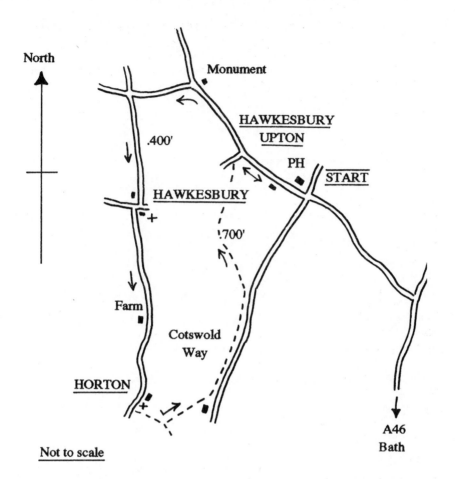

North

Monument

HAWKESBURY
UPTON

.400'

PH
START

HAWKESBURY

.700'

Farm

Cotswold
Way

HORTON

A46
Bath

Not to scale

balcony, lies clearly ahead. Follow the pavement to the monument where, for a modest fee, you can ascend to obtain one of the finest views in the Southern Cotswolds (NB irregular opening hours). Just beyond the monument, the road forks, and yours is the quiet lane to the left, signposted to Wickwar. This lane descends the Cotswold escarpment with a 1 in 6 gradient.

About ½ mile of easy downhill walking brings you to an isolated detached cottage on the right-hand side. Just beyond the cottage, a lane goes off to the right, whilst your route is through the gateway on the left-hand side. This leads on to a bridlepath, which you follow for ½ mile to Hawkesbury. The Landranger map marks this bridlepath as a metalled road, but I doubt very much whether it has seen a road mender since Queen Victoria was on the throne! The bridlepath follows the foot of the Cotswold Edge to Hawkesbury village, with its magnificent church and parsonage, a farmhouse and farm buildings, but little else, all neatly tucked away at the foot of the hillside.

The road bears to the right just past the church, and shortly you turn left along a lane that is followed through to the next village of Horton. This lane is slightly elevated, and each gateway brings quite magnificent views of the Severn Vale, the river and the Forest of Dean. One mile on from Hawkesbury you pass Upper Chalkley Farm, before entering Horton. Having paused to enjoy the delights of Horton church and the adjoining Horton Court, continue through the village until a signpost for the Cotswold Way to Hawkesbury Upton is found by a gateway on the left-hand side.

Pass through this gateway, and follow the path up the hillside to the top left-hand corner of the field. A stile takes you into an area of woodland. Follow the woodland path ahead until, just past a prominent chestnut tree, the Cotswold Way climbs a series of steps on the left-hand side. The path climbs towards the top of the hillside, and follows the edge of the woodland to a stile and out into open fields. Head across the open fields to the hilltop – hundreds of pairs of boots walking the Cotswold Way having made the route pretty obvious.

Just before the hilltop, pass to the left of a stone barn, beyond which the Way begins to run parallel to Highfield Lane, a hedgerow separating the route from the road itself. The footpath follows the hedgerow, crossing an occasional stile into the adjoining field. In ½ mile the Cotswold Way diverges from Highfield Lane to continue along a bridlepath which follows the hilltop back towards Hawkesbury Upton. Below lies the Severn Vale, with the village of Wickwar being especially prominent. Beyond lie the towers of Oldbury Power Station on the banks of the Severn, with the Forest of Dean and the infant Welsh Hills in the far distance. The bridlepath brings you back to the pond on the edge of Hawkesbury Upton, where a right turn takes you through the village and back to the Fox.

Hinton
The Bull

The straggling hamlet of Hinton tends to be overlooked by local guide books, probably on account of its lying within the shadow of the famous National Trust property at nearby Dyrham. Handsome cottages line what was the old Oxford to Bristol coach road, just beneath the Cotswold Edge, and alongside this now quiet byway sits the attractive Bull inn. Fashioned from the local stone, the Bull is indeed an impressive building. In front of it is a paved terrace, complete with picnic tables and sunshades in summer, whilst all around are fine floral displays – tubs, hanging baskets and window boxes. The grey Cotswold stone and the picturesque gabled windows complete a most pleasing vista.

Internally, the Bull offers a public bar and a lounge, all neatly embellished with exposed stonework, black beams and plasterwork. There are a number of dark-wood table and chair sets, together with the rather more traditional pew seats. In the lounge bar is a vast stone fireplace, surrounded by various items of copper and brassware. Around the walls hang further brasses and copper artefacts, together with a number of rustic prints and photos of the Bull. A particularly interesting print displays a sectional map of the old Oxford to Bristol coach road, with Hinton proudly displayed on the approaches to Bristol.

The set menu at the Bull is divided up into a number of sections. These cover ploughman's, open sandwiches (each a 'meal in itself'), omelettes, fish, chicken and steak dishes, plus a good selection of sweets. Regular specials are displayed on a board behind the bar and include, for example, cauliflower cheese, steak and mushroom pie, Stilton omelette, turkey and ham pie, and ham and cheese pasta. The Bull is a Wadworth pub, so it is not surprising to find such brews as 6X and Henry's on offer, as well as a decent Bass beer.

Telephone: 0272 372332.

How to get there: Heading north from Bath on the A46, a left turn is signposted to Hinton, just 1 mile south of the M4 motorway. This unclassified lane drops down the Cotswold escarpment into Hinton, where you will find the Bull on the right-hand side just as you enter the village.

Parking: There is a large car park for patrons in front of the Bull. Otherwise, it is a question of careful roadside parking somewhere in the vicinity of the inn.

Length of the walk: 3 miles. Map: OS Landranger 172 Bristol and Bath (GR 736768).

Despite the lack of miles, this circuit is full of human interest and superb natural landscape. From Hinton, level field paths are followed to the neighbouring village of Dyrham, with the Cotswold escarpment forming a dramatic backdrop. Dyrham itself is home to a magnificent manor house, a 13th century church, a deer park and any number of quaint country cottages. The return to Hinton brings extensive views towards the river Severn and Wales, as the path climbs on to Hinton Hill, site of an ancient hill fort.

The Walk
From the Bull, walk just a few yards down the lane towards Pucklechurch before looking out for a stile in the hedgerow on the left. Actually, it is neither a stile nor a gate, but a cross between the two and not that easy to negotiate. Strangely, there is not one footpath sign between Hinton and Dyrham – careful instructions are vital.

Follow the right-hand hedgerow beyond the stile and, where it ends, continue across the field to a gateway opposite. In the next field, head across to a point where the hedge opposite forms a corner. Continue down the right-hand side of this field boundary to a stile in the corner, beyond which you follow Chapel Lane down past Chapel

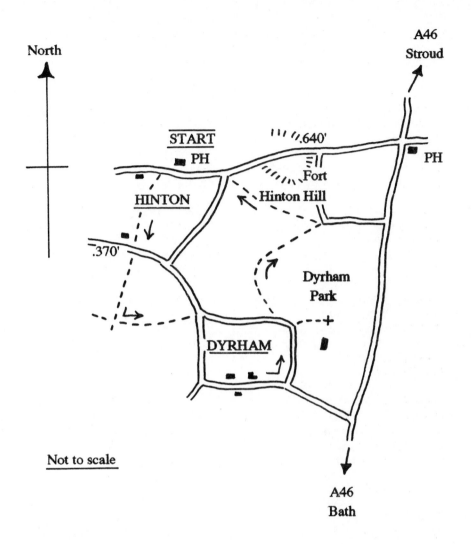

Cottage to the Dyrham to Pucklechurch road.

Cross to a stile the other side of the road, and cross the next field to a gateway in the furthest corner. At this point, the path cuts across a wide enclosed track labelled on the OS sheets as Back Lane. As soon as you have crossed this long-disused track, turn left to a stile/gate. Cross the next field, bearing slightly to the right to reach a stile in the opposite hedgerow, and in the adjacent field follow the long right-hand field boundary all the way to a stile and the Dyrham road. These field paths that cross the level countryside between Hinton and Dyrham bring quite superb views of the Cotswold escarpment rising above Dyrham.

Turn right at the lane and walk past a small waterfall to a road junction where you bear left into the centre of Dyrham. Picturesque cottages line the roadside, with names like Honeysuckle Cottage, Daffodil Cottage and Laburnam Cottage giving a flavour of the place. At the top of the main street, turn left along a lane signposted to the 13th century church. This lane soon brings a superb view of Dyrham House, the mansion built for William Blathwayt, Secretary of State to William III. Just past Dyrham House, a turning on the right leads up to St Mary Magdalene church, a worthwhile detour. The walk itself continues along the lane, past Garden House, before turning right on to the clearly signposted Cotswold Way.

A short climb uphill soon sees the path emerge into open fields. For close on 1 mile, follow the well-worn Cotswold Way as it borders the Dyrham Deer Park. Fine views to the left stretch across the fringes of Bristol to the countryside beyond. The path eventually crosses an arable field to emerge at a gate just before the Hinton to West Littleton road. Do not pass through the gate – rather, stand with your back to the gate and bear right across this arable field towards the trees on the skyline beyond Hinton Hill. This path is signposted by the gateway.

As you approach the far side of the field, the path drops to a hedgerow where a stile brings you out to the right of the field boundary in the neighbouring field. Follow this left-hand boundary on to a second field which lies on the south-facing slopes of Hinton Hill. Two options arise at this stage – either continue across the hillside to the gate at the far side of this overgrown scrubland, or climb to the hilltop on the right and follow the edge of the hill to the same point. The latter option follows what would have been the ramparts of an ancient hill fort and brings magnificent views of the Cotswold Edge, Dyrham Deer Park, the Severn Vale, the Welsh Hills and a whole lot more besides. The gate at the far end of the hillside brings you to the Hinton road. Turn left, and follow Hinton Hill back down to the village, where the Bull shortly appears on the right-hand side.

7. Iron Acton
The White Hart

The White Hart stands at the western end of Iron Acton, casting its gaze the length of the main street through the village. It is a fine street, too, lined with interesting and ancient houses that exude a real sense of history. The White Hart is a sturdy old building, constructed of the local pennant stone, a hard sandstone that was ideally suited for construction work. A good deal of the stonework has now been lost beneath whitewashed plaster, but the mixture of styles produces a pleasing effect. With its gabled roof, its traditional red tiles and its leaded windows, the White Hart presents a picture of a historic village inn. The fact that it was restored as far back as 1892 is testimony to its age.

The bar areas inside the White Hart have a very rustic feel. The black beams and wall panelling, the lanterns around the bar and the walls, the barrel stools and the small wooden tables lend a cosy atmosphere to the inn. Around the walls is hung a collection of photographs and prints, including a number of the Iron Acton area, whilst an extensive selection of old cider pots, ale bottles and china is displayed upon the shelves around the bar. The decidedly rural atmosphere is complemented by items such as hunting boots, barrels and pieces of farm equipment.

The menu at the White Hart includes starters, pies, oven meals, hot and cold platters, 'flare meals', bar snacks, vegetarian meals and sweets. The oven meals are perhaps of greatest interest, with the inn being the proud owner of a unique wood-fired clay stove. The oven dishes are all cooked in this stove, slowly and with delicious marinades. If you are not tempted by a fine cut of lamb or a rib steak, then the whole baby chicken marinated in a honey-based sauce will surely appeal. In addition to the main menu, a daily range of specials is chalked up on a number of chopping boards hung behind the bar. A good range of beers is also available at the White Hart, including Courage Bitter and Directors, Webster's and John Smith's Yorkshire Bitter.

Telephone: 0454 228228.

How to get there: Iron Acton lies halfway between Bristol and Wotton-under-Edge, and is bypassed by the B4058. Follow the signposted lane into the village where the White Hart lies at the western end of the High Street.

Parking: There is a large car park for patrons, alongside the White Hart. There is also ample room for street parking in Iron Acton.

Length of the walk: 4 miles. Map: OS Landranger 172 Bristol and Bath (GR 676837).

This gentle, undulating ramble explores the neighbouring villages of Iron Acton and Frampton Cotterell, as well as short sections of the Frome Valley Walkway. The countryside is pleasant, if unspectacular, with the level of interest being maintained by the unexpected surprises along the way. These include secluded green lanes, delightful riverside paths, old iron workings, a manor house and Chill Wood, a fine patch of deciduous woodland. In an area that has been almost overwhelmed by development, it is pleasing to find such a pleasant rural interlude.

The Walk

At the start of this walk, I will assume that you are parked in Iron Acton's main street. Walk down to the White Hart and turn left, following the pavement for just under ½ mile as far as the B4058 Bristol road. The single track railway crossed en route is the old Thornbury branch line, now used by trains serving Grovesend Quarry. Cross the B4058, and follow the footpath opposite that passes between a group of houses. It is signposted as leading to the Marle Hills. At first this path is a quiet green lane, which shortly joins the driveway leading to Laddenside Farm.

The footpath passes to the left of the farmhouse into open fields. Cross the first two fields, always keeping the hedgerow to your left, until you reach a footbridge that spans Ladden Brook. Follow the right-hand hedgerow in the next field to a gate in the corner where you will join a secluded green lane. Turn left, and follow this

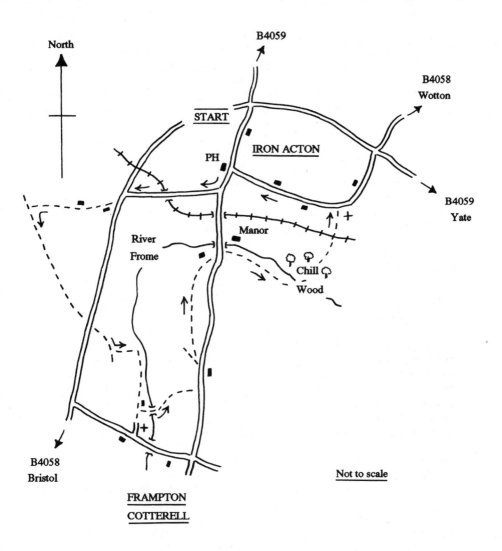

delightful path for ½ mile to the B4058.

Cross the main road with care, and follow the track opposite signposted to Frampton Cotterell. This track soon enters an open field, where you continue alongside the right-hand hedgerow. Where the field widens, bear sharp left and follow a path down towards the trees and the banks of the river Frome. Follow the pleasant riverside path – a section of the Frome Valley Walkway – into Frampton Cotterell.

The path emerges into the village through a contractor's yard. Continue past a bungalow before turning left on to a track just before a group of cottages and St Peter's church. The track crosses the Frome on a flat concrete bridge, before entering open fields. Head straight across to the wooded area opposite, where a pair of awkward stiles lead on to a path that angles up the bank ahead. The area you are entering is the site of the long-disused Roden Acre iron mine, which was last worked in 1874.

At the top of the bank, turn left along a track that was originally a mineral line carrying ore to the main railway at Iron Acton. In just 50 yards, cross the stile on the right-hand side and follow the edge of the wood in the adjoining field. Where the woodland ends, continue across the field in the same direction to a stile beneath a prominent oak tree. Cross the next two fields, aiming for a clearly visible stile in the opposite hedgerow in each case, to emerge on a quiet lane leading from Frampton to Iron Acton.

Turn left along this lane for just 75 yards to a point where the road bears right, a bridlepath bears left, and between them a footpath leads into the fields. Follow this well-defined footpath through the next four fields. The route is well worn, but, just in case, in field 1 cross to the corner of the hedgerow ahead and follow its course to a gate in the corner; in field 2, follow the right-hand field boundary until a stile comes into view in the wall ahead; cross to a stile at the far end of the next field, just to the right of a pylon; in the last field, bear half-right to join the road by the entrance to Brake Farm. Incidentally, these field paths are slightly elevated and bring far-ranging views across the neighbouring countryside. The only drawback is the large number of pylons, all radiating from Oldbury Power Station.

Turn left at the lane, and walk the few yards down to the river Frome alongside Algars Manor. Turn right on to the path signposted to Mayshill, and follow a pretty wooded section of the river bank as far as a waterboard installation. Cross the Frome, and climb the steps into Chill Wood. Despite its rural tranquillity, coal was actually mined in this woodland in the 17th century. Follow the main path through the woodland until you reach an open field. Cut across the corner of this field to a kissing-gate where a path climbs the embankment to cross the railway line encountered at the start of the walk. In the final field, aim for the top left-hand corner, where a stone stile brings you to a path that runs behind a line of houses. This path continues to Iron Acton church and the main street through the village. Turn left at the road, and it is just a few minutes' walk back to the White Hart.

8 Marshfield
The Crown

Marshfield once lay on the historic London to Bristol coach road, with the inns along its High Street offering rest and refreshment to the passing coach trade. The Crown, situated at the eastern end of the main street, was one such local coaching inn. Double-fronted with bay windows, its central archway gave access to the stables at the rear of the inn. Today, Marshfield has been bypassed by the nearby A420, and it is local visitors who form the bulk of the Crown's trade. Anyone coming to this large village cannot fail to be drawn by this 17th century building, with its attractive window boxes and hanging baskets.

Internally, the Crown has been the subject of much renovation since those coaching days, with the accommodation now on offer consisting of the mummers' kitchen, the victuals bar, the stable bar and a most attractive paved courtyard, complete with tables and colourful floral displays. The mummers' kitchen, named after a fertility rite that still takes place in the High Street on Boxing Day mornings, was once a butcher's shop, whilst the cellar beneath the victuals bar was allegedly a onetime local gaol. The furnishings and décor complement this historic picture – dark-wood tables, leather

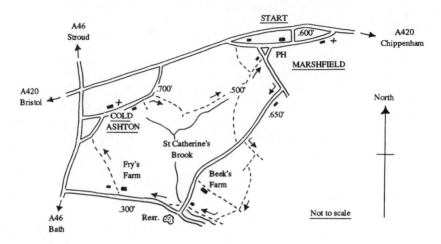

upholstered seats, horse prints, brasses, a vast open fireplace and quite the largest pair of bellows I have ever encountered. Quite naturally, in an inn of such antiquity there is a ghost, and he is said to possess quite a thirst, judging by the ale that mysteriously disappears some nights! Whether his preference is Courage Bitter, Webster's, Triple Crown, Beamish Stout or King and Barnes Broadwood, I cannot say.

An extensive menu consisting of good, home-cooked food is available at the Crown, with all food orders to be given in at the mummers' kitchen just by the entrance. The various headings on the menu include starters, fish, chicken dishes, pizzas, vegetarian dishes, charcoal grills, salads, sandwiches, omelettes, pies, childrens' dishes and sweets. There is so much to recommend. From the fish dishes, salmon with prawn and mushroom sauce might prove tempting, or perhaps the country farer's steak from the charcoal grills. The various steak pies, with their crisp puff pastry, are equally appealing, as is the grilled chicken served with a delicious barbecue sauce. The irresistible sweets menu includes fruit pie with fresh cream, sorbets, gâteaux and a selection of French ices. One thing is certain – you will soon replace those calories lost on the walk.

Telephone: 0225 891189.

How to get there: Marshfield lies just off the A420 Bristol to Chippenham road, 3 miles east of its junction with the A46. Turn off the A420 into the village, where the Crown is at the eastern end of the High Street.

Parking: There is plenty of roadside parking in the vicinity of the Crown.

40

Length of the walk: 7 miles. Map: OS Landranger 172 Bristol and Bath (GR 780738).

Marshfield is an isolated stone village, high on the Cotswold ridge, that is literally strung along one main street. Its heyday was in the coaching era, since when it has retired into a period of quiet gentility. To the south of the village lies a network of steep hills and secluded valleys that carry tributary streams down to the Avon at Bath. The walk explores this quite spectacular landscape, centred upon the beautiful St Catherine's Valley. The return to Marshfield sees our steps pass through the neighbouring hilltop village of Cold Ashton, where a Jacobean manor house sits proudly overlooking the head of the valley. Admittedly a strenuous excursion, but one that will linger long in the memory.

The Walk

From the Crown, head westwards along Marshfield's High Street, past the Catherine Wheel Inn and the village post office, before turning left into Sheepfair Lane. In a few hundred yards, turn left at the junction with St Martin's Lane and continue out of Marshfield as far as the village cricket ground on the left-hand side. Opposite the cricket club, turn right into Beek's Lane, a quiet cul-de-sac that heads nowhere in particular and has a traffic volume to match. Continue along Beek's Lane for ½ mile, with views into a secluded valley on the right-hand side. Shortly after the lane descends the hillside, turn left on to a signposted bridlepath.

Continue along this secluded bridlepath for 300 yards to a point where there is a stile in the right-hand hedgerow. Cross this stile into an open field, and follow the right-hand hedgerow across the hilltop. In the far corner of the field, you will reach a stile beyond which the path should descend to Beek's Cottage, according to the OS sheets. Avon County Council has diverted the path, however, a diversion that probably means greater privacy for the residents but which also brings quite superb views for ramblers.

Beyond the stile, turn left and follow the field boundary all of the way around to the far left-hand corner of the field. Quite superb views down into St Catherine's Valley open up as you walk alongside the left-hand field boundary. Cross the stile in the corner of this field, and again follow the left-hand field boundary across the next field to a stile in the corner and a track leading to Beek's Cottage. Cross this track to a stile directly opposite and, in the next field, bear half-right to a stile halfway down the right-hand hedgerow. In the next field, head downhill towards a stile in the right-hand corner. You are now right in the depths of St Catherine's Valley, surrounded by sweeping hillsides – a magnificent vista.

Cross the stile, and follow the footpath across the bottom of the

41

next two fields as it runs parallel to St Catherine's Brook on your left. The path emerges on the lane leading to Beek's Farm. Cross this lane, follow the signposted footpath opposite into an adjoining field and bear left to climb a steep ridge that leads to a gateway and the lane running through the valley. Turn right, and follow this quiet byway for ½ mile as far as Fry's Farm.

Between the farmhouse and the outbuildings, follow the bridlepath on the right-hand side. This secluded green lane eventually passes across a couple of fields before joining Slough Lane. Turn right at the lane and continue uphill to Cold Ashton village. Turn right when you reach the main road through the village, which passes the quite magnificent Jacobean manor house on the left-hand side, at the head of St Catherine's Valley. A short distance past the last cottage in the village, a signposted footpath appears on the right-hand side. Continue past this right of way for just 200 yards to a second signed footpath, on the right, that heads downhill into a marvellously secluded valley.

This path initially heads across the middle of an open field to the opposite corner, where you will find a gateway beneath a group of trees. Beyond this gateway, continue downhill through a narrow tributary valley into the main valley bottom. When you reach a cross track, turn left past a ruinous dwelling to another gateway and meadows that line the valley bottom. The directions for the next mile of walking make tedious reading, but contrast vividly with the splendid landscape in this valley – one of the most secluded in the area.

In the first field, the path contours across the hillside to a gateway opposite, all the while running parallel to the valley bottom. Continue across the second field, gradually descending to reach a handgate in the far right-hand corner. Follow the right-hand field boundary alongside the stream bed through a third field, as far as a stile in what looks like a piece of temporary fencing. In the fourth and final field, continue to the far right-hand corner where the path climbs to a stile to join a green lane. Turn left along this for just 100 yards. Where the bridlepath bears sharply to the left, cross the stile ahead into an open field. Follow the right-hand hedgerow to a stile in the corner, and in the next field bear half-left to pass in front of the large detached house on the skyline. A stile brings you on to St Martin's Lane where you turn left to reach Marshfield's main street. Turn right to return to the Crown.

9 Hanham Mills
The Chequers Inn

Hanham Mills lies in a deep, wooded valley just beyond the eastern fringes of Bristol. The river Avon at this point is navigable, with pleasure craft making a pleasant waterside scene for the visitor. In the past, commercial traffic would have plied its trade along the river – Shropshire coal going upstream towards Bath, with Bath stone being shipped down to Bristol. The Chequers Inn lies on the river bank, and was once the watering hole of these thirsty bargees who worked the Avon. Although it has been the subject of much renovation in recent years, the traditional bargees would still recognise the Chequers' exterior, fashioned from the local pennant sandstone.

Internally, the Chequers has been extensively but tastefully modernised. Wood panelling is the order of the day, whether on the walls, the ceilings or the partitions that divide the main bar into a number of levels. With its carpeted floors, imitation oil lamps and dark-wood table and chair sets, the Chequers offers the visitor a comfortable welcome. It is the riverside location, however, that is the main attraction of the inn. Picture windows in both the lounge and dining area provide fine views of the river, whilst the tables on the balcony outside provide an even better outlook. A number of picnic tables are also located on the river bank, alongside a children's play area, to make the best use of the inn's beautiful situation.

A carvery in the main bar offers a good range of hot meals to visitors. These include a selection of pies – steak and kidney, steak and mushroom, lamb and leek, chicken and broccoli, mushroom and nut. The Chequers can also offer lasagne, steaks, curries, burgers and a range of ploughman's lunches. If you wish to eat in style, the restaurant attached to the inn offers waitress service in a dining area with quite superb views of the river. The Chequers is a freehouse, with a range of beers and ales to match, for example, Ruddles, Courage Bitter, Wadworth 6X and Simonds Bitter, as well as a selection of lagers.

The Chequers is a busy inn on account of its riverside location in the vicinity of a large urban area. It may not enjoy the relaxed, quiet atmosphere of many country pubs, but it does offer a friendly and hospitable welcome to all visitors. On a warm summer's evening, the river bank alongside the inn, with pleasure craft cruising the Avon and the sound of birdsong in the woods, is an ideal place at which to enjoy a pint.

Telephone: 0272 674242.

How to get there: The A431 runs from Bath to Bristol to the north of the river Avon, through Kelston, Bitton and Longwell Green. About ½ mile west of its junction with the A4175 Keynsham road, turn left into Court Farm Road. In just over 1 mile, a turning on the left is signposted to the Chequers Inn. The inn lies at the bottom of this cul-de-sac lane, alongside the river Avon.

Parking: As you drive into Hanham Mills, there is a large parking area on the left opposite the Chequers Inn.

Length of the walk: 3 ½ miles. Map: OS Landranger 172 Bristol and Bath (GR 648701).

Despite being just a few miles from the centre of Bristol, the river Avon between Hanham and Keynsham manages to retain a remarkably rural feel. The river passes through a wooded valley and meadowland, where the hustle and bustle of the nearby city is soon forgotten. From this riverside pub, we explore the towpath alongside the navigable waterway, as well as the neighbouring woodland. Other features of interest include the pleasure craft on the river, Hanham Lock and Hanham Court.

The Walk
From the Chequers Inn, follow the towpath westwards (to the right) as the river plunges into a wooded valley. In ¼ mile, the path passes

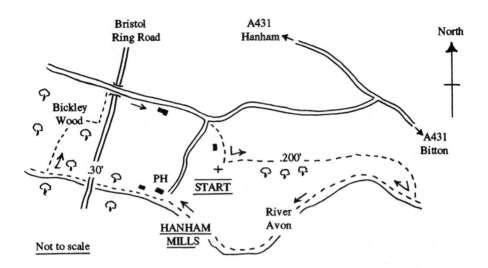

beneath the vast bridge that carries the Avon Ring Road across the valley. In another ¼ mile, look out for a footpath on the right-hand side, signposted 'Elm Tree PH'.

Turn right, and follow this path up through Bickley Wood and away from the river. There are many paths in the woods, but stick to the main route that steadily climbs the hillside, occasional flights of steps reassuring you that you are on the official right of way. This woodland is delightfully lonely and secluded, a superb area of deciduous tree-cover and the occasional rocky outcrop.

In less than ½ mile, after a short descent down a flight of steps, cross the footbridge that appears on the right-hand side. This takes you across a small stream that tumbles down to the Avon. Once across the bridge, turn left for a few yards before turning right on to a path that climbs out of the woods to a stile and an open field. Follow the left-hand field boundary ahead until you run up against the Avon Ring Road, which has rather inconveniently severed the footpath. Turn left, following the path up to the road bridge across the ring road.

Turn right at the road, and walk for 280 yards to a triangular green where a right-hand fork leaves Court Farm Road for the Chequers. Head straight across this green, between the two roads, to a kissing-gate in the wall ahead. Once through this gateway, cross the field ahead to reach the driveway that runs past Hanham Court and down to the neighbouring church.

Just before you reach the church, look out for an iron gate on the left and a signposted footpath leading to Willsbridge. Follow the enclosed path beyond this gate as far as a kissing-gate and open fields.

45

Head straight across the first field, beyond which you follow the edge of Cleeve Wood virtually all of the way down to the river Avon. This slightly elevated section of the walk brings fine views towards Bath, with Kelston Round Hill being especially prominent – the hilltop has an unmistakable clump of trees.

Where the woodland ends, a short section of green lane takes you down to the river bank. The stonework a few yards along the bank to your left at this point marks the site of Londonderry Wharf. A tramline once ran down to the river from nearby collieries, and the coal was loaded on to barges at this point. Our route, however, lies in the opposite direction from the wharf site. We now follow the river bank for just over 1 mile. No longer is the river running through a deep wooded valley, rather it follows a meandering course across meadowland. On the opposite bank of the river, the vast red-brick Cadbury's factory is one landmark you will not miss! Built in 1923, the original factory had been sited in central Bristol. This was an early case of relocation to a greenfield site. A leisurely stroll across the fields brings you back to the Chequers Inn.

 Saltford
The Jolly Sailor

The Jolly Sailor is a real waterside inn, sitting alongside Saltford Lock on the river Avon. The inn dates from 1726 and is contemporary with the opening of the Avon Navigation. The bargees literally left their mark upon the Jolly Sailor – if you examine the fireplace in the lounge, the wooden surround will be found to be riddled with holes. It was the custom at the time for any newly promoted barge captain to pick up a red-hot poker from the fire to bore a hole into the wood before buying a round of drinks for his crew. This was not the only act of vandalism in the vicinity of the Jolly Sailor – the local Somerset miners were so incensed at the arrival of imported Shropshire coal along the Avon that they destroyed Saltford Lock. Above the same fireplace hangs a painting of the local riverside scene before this act of destruction.

The Jolly Sailor is a delightful Courage inn. The large stone building fronts the river, with magnificent views across Saltford Lock and the neighbouring weir. There can be few more pleasant watering holes around Bath and Bristol than the Jolly Sailor on a balmy summer's evening – sitting alongside the river with rolling hills in the distance and the waterside activity close at hand. If you can resist the small garden overlooking the river, you will find an attractive interior to the inn. The stone-walled bar and snug contain original fireplaces and paintings, whilst the recently constructed conservatory provides a bright and airy dining-room.

The Jolly Sailor offers good traditional pub fare. The bar menu contains all the favourites – soups, sandwiches, ploughman's and salads – whilst each day a range of special dishes is displayed on a blackboard. These include a vegetarian dish. As this is a Courage inn, the spotlight is on beers such as Courage Best and Directors, although other fine ales such as John Smith's Bitter are available.

Telephone: 0225 873002.

How to get there: Saltford is on the A4 between Bath and Bristol. From the main road, follow the signs to the Bath and Bristol Cyclepath. The road passes another pub – the Bird in the Hand – before going under the cyclepath (an old railway line). There is a parking place on the right just by the railway bridge. The Jolly Sailor lies another ½ mile along this cul-de-sac road, which is called Mead Lane. The walk starts from the railway bridge and it is best to park there, driving on to the pub for refreshment later.

Parking: There is a large car park for patrons at the Jolly Sailor, and room to leave your car by the railway bridge while you walk.

Length of the walk: 4½ miles. Map: OS Landranger 172 Bristol and Bath (GR 687675 start of walk, 693679 Jolly Sailor).

A quite magnificent walk, which lies at the southern end of the Cotswolds, where the hillside slopes come tumbling down to the banks of the river Avon. This excursion climbs on to the hills, where a marvellously secluded bridlepath follows the hillside slopes. Tucked away in a fold in the hills lies the isolated village of North Stoke, so lonely and remote despite its proximity to close on 1 million people! From the breezy hilltops, the route descends to the water's edge where our footsteps follow the river bank back into Saltford.

The Walk
Alongside the parking area, a path slopes gently up to the Bath and Bristol Cyclepath. Follow the cyclepath the short distance across the river Avon. About 100 yards beyond the bridge, descend the flight of steps on the left-hand side. Cross the stile at the foot of the embankment and turn left along an enclosed farm track. Beyond a gateway, this well-defined track crosses two fields, before passing through a scattered collection of farm buildings on to the main A431 road in the village of Kelston. The village sits against a backdrop of the

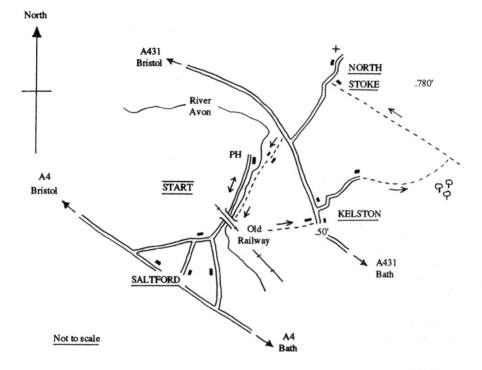

North

A431
Bristol

River
Avon

PH

START

A4
Bristol

Old
Railway

Not to scale

SALTFORD

+

NORTH

STOKE

.780'

KELSTON

.50'

A431
Bath

A4
Bath

southern slopes of the Cotswold Hills, with the clump of trees atop Kelston Round Hill being the most prominent landmark.

Turn left, follow the pavement past the Crown Inn to the edge of the village, where you turn right on to an unmarked lane that heads towards the hills. This metalled byway climbs for ½ mile to Coomb Barn, an isolated farm complex with far-reaching views across the Avon valley. The lane passes to the right in front of the barn, and continues its ceaseless climb towards the hilltop. Very soon it becomes an unmetalled bridlepath, enclosed between a pair of hedgerows. Some 600 yards on from Coomb Barn, look out for the point where the bridlepath stops climbing and bears to the left to follow a level course across the hillside. In the hedgerow on the right at this bend, you will see a stile which leads on to a permissive path, heading to the summit of Kelston Round Hill. This is an energetic detour, but one that is well worth making for the fine views that it brings across Bath and Bristol. Back on the route itself, continue along the hillside path for just under ½ mile to a cross track.

Turn left at this junction and follow a wonderfully secluded bridlepath across the hillside for close on 1 mile, into the village of

North Stoke. The views from this path are superb and, being on the level, can be appreciated fully.

To explore the village itself, including the delightful St Martin's church, a detour to the right is needed as you enter North Stoke. Retrace your steps to this point to continue the walk.

Turn left as you come into North Stoke to follow a quiet lane back downhill to the A431. Turn right, follow the pavement for a few yards, and then cross a stile in the hedgerow on the left-hand side. Head across the field beyond, with the river Avon a short distance to the right. Cross a stream and a stile into the next field, where you make for the complex of buildings ahead that make up the hamlet of Kelston Mill. This was the site of a brass foundry during the 18th and 19th centuries.

Pass to the right of the tall row of workers' cottages – between their front doors and their gardens – cross a stile and make for the river bank. The Jolly Sailor lies on the far bank of the Avon, but short of mustering up some supernatural powers, there is still some walking left! Continue along the river bank for ½ mile until you reach the steel-girder bridge across the Avon, crossed at the outset. Climb the steep path up the embankment to the cyclepath, recross the Avon and return to your vehicle parked just below. It is now just a question of a short drive along Mead Lane to the Jolly Sailor . . . and that well-deserved drink.

Bathampton
The George

Bathonians have for many years enjoyed this inn's fine location alongside the towpath of the Kennet and Avon Canal. Although the sign on the wall of the George dates the current building as *c.* 1840, the history books would tell a far different story. This was originally a hostelry for the ancient priory of Hampton, with origins that could go back as far as the 14th century. Intriguingly, underground passages are thought to link the inn with the neighbouring church and vicarage – and the connections run further. Viscount du Barry, victim of the last legal duel fought in Britain and now buried in the nearby churchyard, was laid out for his wake in one of the inn's lounges.

Internally, the George is an interesting collection of stone, low-ceilinged rooms, with beams, horse brasses, old rifles, oil paintings and sherry barrels. The atmosphere is decidedly historic and traditional. It is the food, however, for which the George has earned an enviable reputation. There is a large set menu, which includes vegetarian dishes, as well as a number of specials, with such tempting choices as pork in blackberry and orange, chicken Stroganov, salmon and asparagus quiche, and chicken and broccoli bake on offer. This is in addition to the staple fare of pubs – salads, ploughman's and sandwiches. The sweets are equally inviting and include chocolate fudge pudding, Caribbean pancake, and pineapple and custard flan. Thirsts can be quenched with one of a number of fine beers including Courage Best, Bass and Irish Beamish, whilst a good selection of wines is listed on the wine menu.

The George is very popular, with its canalside location and delightful garden attracting large numbers of walkers, cyclists, bargees and motorists. Being so close to the city of Bath, it is equally popular as a lunchtime watering hole with the local business community. A relaxed and friendly ambience is the order of the day at this fine old inn, crowds or no crowds.

Telephone: 0225 425079.

How to get there: Leave Bath on the A36 Warminster road. Less than 2 miles out from the city centre, an unclassified road on the left-hand side – Bathampton Lane – leads down to Bathampton village. Follow this road through the village, and across the Kennet and Avon Canal, and the George is on the left-hand side.

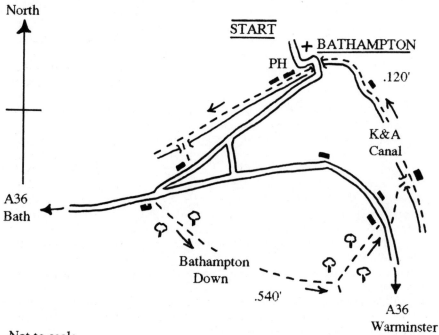

North

START

+ BATHAMPTON

PH

.120'

K&A
Canal

A36
Bath

Bathampton
Down

.540'

A36
Warminster

Not to scale

52

Parking: There is a large car park for patrons, to the rear of the George. There is also plenty of room for roadside parking in Tyning Road, adjacent to the inn and alongside the canal.

Length of the walk: 3 miles. Map: OS Landranger 172 Bristol and Bath, Pathfinder 66/76 Bath and Keynsham (GR 776665).

This short excursion on the north-eastern fringes of Bath is a walk of vivid contrasts. From the relaxed and gentle Kennet and Avon canal towpath, a strenuous climb follows on to Bathampton Down. The views from the hilltop are quite superb, dominated by the Avon valley as it loops majestically into the city of Bath. A steep descent along an old mineral tramline − Bathampton Down was the source of much of the building stone used in Bath − brings our steps back to the canal and Bathampton village. St Nicholas's church is worth a visit, not only to discover the tomb of the last victim of a legal duel fought on English soil, but also to view the chapel erected to the memory of Admiral Arthur Phillip, the first Governor of New South Wales.

The Walk
From the George, follow the canal towpath westwards for ½ mile to the first over-bridge − Candy's Bridge. Leave the canal at this point, cross the bridge and follow the lane ahead uphill to join Bathampton Lane. Turn right, and continue uphill to the busy A36 trunk road.

Cross the main road with care, and follow the footpath opposite, uphill, for over ¼ mile. This is a steep climb, but the trees afford the luxury of some shade and shelter from the elements. You emerge onto the open hilltop, Bathampton Down, which is common land with a seemingly endless number of paths. Describing the route is easier than actually finding it! The OS Pathfinder map would be an asset here − aim for GR 777654. Once you emerge out of the trees near the hilltop, continue climbing the slope in front until you reach the open hilltop. A prominent aerial stands 250 yards away to your right. Bear left, and follow the airy hilltop towards the trees some 200 yards distant. The fine view on your left encompasses the Avon valley, Solsbury Hill, Brown's Folly and a deal more besides − that Pathfinder map could double up as your topograph.

As you approach the woods, bear slightly to the right, climbing the gentle slope towards a yellow flag marking one of the greens on the neighbouring golf course. The 'path' enters the woodland about 20 yards down from the golf course boundary fence. Continue along the woodland path for 250 yards to a metal stile, beyond which a cross track is reached. Turn left, and follow the steep incline all the way down to the A36. This is the bed of the old tramline that once carried stone from the Bathampton Down quarries down to the Kennet and

Avon Canal for shipment to Bath. Incidentally, that trusty Pathfinder map would enable you to seek out a detour on the hilltops to discover the old quarries where one or two mine workings can still be explored with care.

When you reach the A36, cross to the pavement opposite and follow the road to the right for a short distance. Where the road bears to the right, cross a stile on the left to follow what is still the incline down to Hampton Wharf on the canal. This part of the walk brings a fine view of the Avon valley, with the river, the canal, the Southampton railway and the A36 all following a parallel course – living evidence of the history of transport. Cross the canal by means of the footbridge at the wharf, turn left and follow the towpath back into Bathampton. This level finale will certainly come as welcome relief after the descent from Bathampton Down.

12 Lacock
The Red Lion

Lacock has been described as 'easily the most remarkable and the most beautiful village in Wiltshire'. Based around four streets – Church Street, West and East Streets and the High Street – Lacock still very much resembles a medieval town. The Red Lion's seven bays, three storeys high, stand impressively at the junction of the High Street with East Street. As if to remind the visitor that Lacock sits at the geological divide between limestone country and the clay vale of the Avon, the inn's red-brick frontage is faced with blocks of golden Bath stone.

The Red Lion, a fine 18th century hostelry, exudes a traditional rural atmosphere, with its open-plan interior being divided into smaller, more intimate areas by a mixture of cart shafts, yokes and other agricultural implements. The walls display a fascinating collection of memorabilia, including plates, oil paintings, prints and tools, whilst stuffed birds, animals and branding irons hang from the ceilings. Jugs and pots of dried flowers deck the window sills and shelves. Completing the picture are the partly flagstoned floor, Turkey rugs and a blazing log fire in winter. To the rear is a small garden, complete with a number of picnic tables, whilst the inn's old stable block now functions as a tearoom.

The bar food has a deservedly good reputation, with a blackboard displaying the ever-changing array of dishes. These include Lacock beef pie, Wiltshire duck with orange and brandy sauce, a brace of giant sausages, beef, mushroom and ale pie, pork, apple and cider, and chicken and pepper bake. The range of puddings is equally rich and varied. Being a Wadworth house, the fine beers brewed nearby in Devizes are available – IPA, 6X, Farmer's Glory and Old Timer – with good wines available by the glass.

Telephone: 0249 730766.

How to get there: Lacock lies just ½ mile off the main A350 Chippenham to Melksham road. The Red Lion is at the eastern end of the High Street, almost opposite the entrance to Lacock Abbey.

Parking: Signposts lead visitors to Lacock to a free car park which is just two minutes' walk from the Red Lion. Walk directions will therefore be based upon this visitors' car park. There is also a patrons' car park alongside the Red Lion.

Length of the walk: 2½ miles. Map: OS Landranger 173 Swindon and Devizes (GR 917684).

Lacock, deep in the Wiltshire countryside, is a National Trust village of international repute. The medieval street plan, the local abbey, the church and a host of magnificent buildings attract thousands of visitors each year. Whilst the village itself could easily fill several hours of your time, this walk also provides the opportunity to explore the river Avon as it meanders across the local floodplain from Reybridge.

The Walk
Turn right along the road on leaving the car park, heading out into the countryside and away from the village. Use the pavement alongside the sometimes busy Devizes Road, which follows the southern boundary wall of the abbey grounds. After a few hundred yards, a causeway carries the path over the Avon's floodplain, before a stone bridge crosses the river itself. As there is no pavement on the bridge, extreme care needs to be taken. Just past the bridge, cross a stile in the wall on the left, into the adjoining field.

Bear slightly to the right across this first field, aiming for a telegraph pole in the hedgerow opposite. Cross the stile at this point, and head straight across the next, much smaller, field to a gateway in the opposite hedgerow. In the third field, cross to another telegraph pole, next to which is a gate. Once past this gateway, the river Avon comes into view a few yards below.

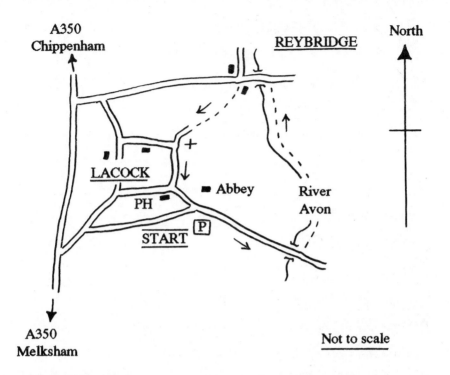

A350
Chippenham

A350
Melksham

REYBRIDGE

North

LACOCK

PH

Abbey

River
Avon

START   P

Not to scale

Keeping the Avon on your left, follow the riverside path all the way through to Reybridge, where a stile is crossed on to the road. Turn left, crossing the river on an attractive stone bridge. A row of pretty thatched cottages will immediately face you at the road junction at the far side of the bridge. Here you should turn left.

Pass between the pair of cottages on the left, where the road bears to the right. Follow the tarmac path through a gate and across the fields back towards Lacock. At the far end of the path, turn left down the lane, and continue on into Lacock. Cross Bide Brook on the pack-horse bridge next to the ford. Returning to Lacock, turn right into Church Street, and then first left into East Street. The Red Lion faces you at the top of the road, with the car park just minutes away to the left.

13 Semington
The Somerset Arms

The Somerset Arms sits alongside the busy A350, a couple of miles south of Melksham. Today's traffic and the passing trade it brings to this Ushers hostelry in one sense reflects the inn's history. The Somerset Arms was a coaching inn as far back as the 16th century, when horse-drawn trade from perhaps London to Wells, or Poole to Chippenham would have passed through the vicinity.

The inn is a pleasing mixture of local stone, red brick and whitewashed walls, with a beer garden to the rear, well away from the main road. Internally, there is a heavily beamed main bar, with an adjoining lounge and dining area. Around the walls are displayed a range of prints and photographs, brassware, a case of stuffed woodpeckers and a number of farm tools. Many of the photographs provide a fascinating insight into life on the nearby Kennet and Avon Canal in years gone by. The combination of open and flame-effect fires in winter, high-backed settles and wooden tables creates a welcoming atmosphere.

Alongside the bar are chalked up the day's bar meals. These might include steak and kidney pie, beef and ale pie, seafood platter or vegetable lasagne. There is also the regular restaurant menu, with its starters, steaks and grills, poultry, fish and vegetarian meals. Traditionalists might opt for the 8 oz sirloin steak or the mixed grill, whilst the more adventurous palates might be tempted by the breaded chicken tikka masala or the mushroom and nut fettuccine. Needless to say, there is a good selection of sweets on offer, including sorbets, raspberry meringues and banana brandy snaps. To quench your thirst, a range of beers is available, including Ushers BB, Wadworth 6X and Old Timer, and Ruddles.

Telephone: 0225 870067.

How to get there: Semington lies on the A350, just 2 miles south of Melksham. The Somerset Arms is on the main road through the village, just ¼ mile south of the humped-back bridge across the Kennet and Avon Canal.

Parking: There is a large car park for patrons, behind the Somerset Arms. Roadside parking can be found in the side roads just below the inn, such as Church Street and Pound Lane. These are residential areas, however, so park with consideration.

Length of the walk: 5 miles. Map: OS Landranger 173 Swindon and Devizes (GR 897606).

Semington is an interesting village with many fine 18th century houses, rather spoiled by the traffic. This walk explores the countryside to the west of the village, where secluded bridlepaths and quiet lanes cross a pleasant, undulating landscape. Along the way we find the isolated hamlet of Whaddon, with its lonely church overlooking the Avon valley. The return to Semington follows a quiet section of the Kennet and Avon Canal, with a little-known aqueduct and a fine pair of locks.

The Walk
From the Somerset Arms, follow the A350 southwards for just ¼ mile, before turning right into St George's Road, where signposts bear the legend 'St George's Hospital'. Continue along this quiet side road as far as the hospital, whose forbidding appearance betrays its original function as the local workhouse. The road ends at the hospital, where the right of way continues across the countryside as a potentially

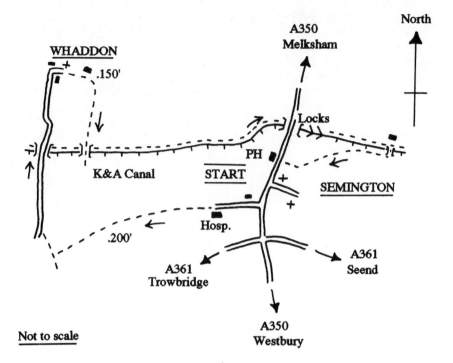

North

WHADDON

A350
Melksham

.150'

Locks

K&A Canal

PH

START

SEMINGTON

Hosp.

.200'

A361
Trowbridge

A361
Seend

A350
Westbury

Not to scale

muddy bridlepath. Follow this bridlepath westwards, enjoying the open views of the Wiltshire countryside to the north. In 1 mile, at a junction, bear right for 100 yards along another bridlepath to join the Hilperton to Whaddon lane.

Turn right, and follow this quiet byway through to Whaddon, crossing the Kennet and Avon Canal en route. Whaddon is a tiny hamlet, consisting of a few farms and poultry houses, an isolated church and little else. The small ecclesiastical building, crafted of local stone, sits on the hilltop overlooking the Avon valley below. Follow the lane to the right through Whaddon, past the church, and on as far as Whaddon Grove Farm. Just before the farmhouse, turn right on to a muddy track that crosses a couple of fields to reach the Kennet and Avon Canal at Whaddon Grove Bridge, with Hill Farm perched on the hillside ahead. Turn left and follow the canal for over 1 mile back to the A350, passing a swingbridge and crossing Semington Aqueduct on the way. The aqueduct crossing Semington Brook is an impressive, though squat, structure. Follow the canal beneath the main road, past Buckley's and Barrett's locks and on as far as another swingbridge. Incidentally, the slight widening of the canal immediately beyond the

A350 is the site of its junction with the old Wiltshire and Berkshire Canal.

Cross the swingbridge, and follow the opposite bank of the canal back towards Semington through the adjoining field. In the much larger field beyond, bear half-left. Your target is a footbridge across Semington Brook, down in the bottom left-hand corner of the field. Once across this footbridge, aim for a stile in the far right-hand corner of the next field. Beyond this stile, bear right, aiming for a footpath that runs behind the chalet bungalows at the far side of the field. This path emerges onto the A350, across the road from the Somerset Arms.

14 Farleigh Hungerford
The Hungerford Arms

The Hungerford family dominate the history of this corner of northeast Somerset. Sir Thomas Hungerford was the first speaker of the House of Commons way back in 1383, and his mortal remains lie in the ancestral home – the chapel that is within the ruins of the local castle. Where landed aristocracy hold such sway within a community, it is not surprising to find that even the village hostelry pays its allegiance to the local gentry.

The Hungerford Arms is an attractive stone building, located on the hillside above the Frome valley. Whilst its frontage on to the busy A366 might appear initially somewhat uninspiring, the view from the rear of the inn could hardly be more delightful. The gardens and picnic tables overlook the river Frome deep in its valley, surrounded by rolling hillsides and woodland. This is a historic landscape, for it was through this valley in 1644 that the Parliamentary forces poured to lay siege to the Royalists garrisoned in Farleigh Castle. This historic picture continues inside the inn, where the visitor will find black beams, timber panelled walls and magnificent stone fireplaces. Above each fireplace in the lounge is displayed the Hungerford coat of arms, leaving patrons in no doubt as to the dynasty that lurks in the neighbourhood. Beyond the lounge bar lies the inn's restaurant, whilst the garden lobby provides a welcome respite should the weather turn inclement for customers using the outdoor facilities. The lounge itself is divided into a number of more intimate areas by attractive partitions, constructed of beams, plaster and coloured glass.

The menu at the Hungerford Arms offers patrons starters, bar meals, fish dishes, salads, Farleigh potatoes, ploughman's, grills, children's dishes and sweets. In addition, a constantly changing range of special dishes is displayed on blackboards alongside the bar. A particularly tasty starter is crispy seafood, whilst on the fish menu the local Farleigh trout will certainly catch the eye. Pork loin chops from the grills is another tempting option, as is the Farleigh jacket potato filled with Stilton and ham. The sweets seem custom-made to restore all of those calories waylaid on the walk, with raspberry pavlova and banana longboat sure to tempt even the most disciplined of palates. Being a traditional West Country pub, good local beers are always available at the Hungerford Arms. These might include various Ushers or Wadworth brews, with the latter's 6X always proving an irresistible pint.

Telephone: 0225 752411.

How to get there: Farleigh Hungerford lies 3 miles west of Trowbridge on the A366 Radstock road. The Hungerford Arms fronts the main road, just a short distance from Farleigh Castle.

Parking: Although the Hungerford Arms has a patrons' car park, it is perhaps more considerate when out walking to park at Farleigh Castle, just minutes' walk from the inn. Do check and see when this car park is locked, however.

Length of the walk: 6 miles. Map: OS Landranger 172 Bristol and Bath and 173 Swindon and Devizes (GR 800575).

There is just so much of interest on this circuit that to condense it into a few lines of description is wholly inadequate. The natural landscape is formed by the lower reaches of the Somerset Frome as it joins the Bristol Avon. The rivers dissect their way through the Somerset and Wiltshire countryside, forming a marvellous network of hillsides and valleys. The villages on the walk — Farleigh Hungerford, Westwood, Avoncliff, Freshford and Iford — contain buildings that will have the architectural enthusiast simply drooling — manor houses, a castle, traditional cloth mills, fine bridges, first-rate farmhouses. One local author has described the area as 'the nearest England gets to the Loire valley'.

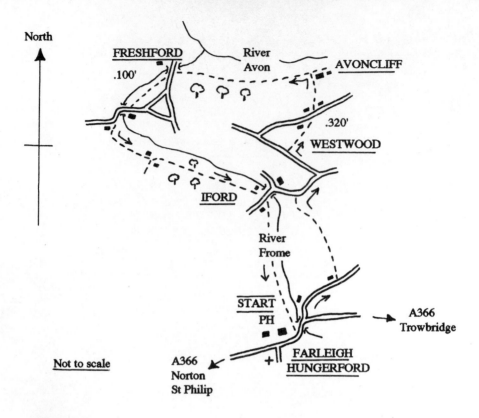

North

FRESHFORD
.100'

River
Avon

AVONCLIFF

.320'

WESTWOOD

IFORD

River
Frome

START

PH

A366
Trowbridge

Not to scale

A366
Norton
St Philip

FARLEIGH
HUNGERFORD

The Walk

The route starts from the car park at Farleigh Castle. The rectangular building, with its circular towers, fortifications and gatehouse, dating from the 1370s and built by Sir Thomas Hungerford, was garrisoned by the Royalists in 1644. Skirmishes at the time left it in a somewhat parlous state. From the ruinous castle remains, follow the A366 in the direction of Trowbridge. Cross the Frome and its adjoining millstream, before bearing left on to an unclassified lane signposted to Westwood. In ¼ mile, having tackled a not insubstantial hill, bear left on to a muddy bridlepath just beyond an isolated bungalow.

In a little over ¼ mile, the path reaches a stream before bearing to the left to continue on to Iford Hill. Turn right, and climb the 1 in 5 incline to reach the Westwood to Freshford road. Turn left at the junction (towards Freshford), and in ¼ mile turn right on to a bridlepath, signposted to Upper Westwood. Turn right at the road in Upper Westwood and, in just 25 yards, left on to an unmetalled lane alongside a cottage.

This lane ends at a gate. Beyond the gate, follow the right-hand field boundary downhill for 100 yards to a stile, pausing to enjoy the fine views of the Avon valley below. Steps lead down to a sunken path, which continues downhill to another stile. Follow the field path to Avoncliff, emerging to the left of the Old Court. Somewhat ironically, this former workhouse has now been converted into upmarket housing units.

Detour to the right at this point if you wish to explore Avoncliff, where the Cross Guns Inn sits alongside a fine aqueduct on the Kennet and Avon Canal.

To continue the walk, turn left along an enclosed path to reach a stile and the river Avon. Follow the river bank across an open field and along the edge of Avoncliff Wood to a second field. Aim for the road at the far corner of this field, just to the left of the inn at Freshford. The bridge at this point crosses the sparkling waters of the Frome, a tributary of the Avon.

Turn left, and follow the Westwood road for 100 yards to a gate/stile on the right. Field paths cross two fields to reach the Peradin factory, housed in the old Dunkirk woollen mill. Turn right, following the road alongside the factory and across the Frome, before turning left on to a bridlepath alongside Dunkirk Mill Cottage. Bear left in front of Middle House to follow this path across the hillside above the Frome.

In ½ mile you reach the isolated hamlet of Friary, once the home of the lay brothers from nearby Hinton Priory. Beyond a handgate, the path descends to a lane before continuing opposite the cottage on your left, Whistlers Hollow, to an open field and Friary Wood. Continue through the woodland to a large riverside meadow, where you aim for the far right-hand corner, almost ½ mile distant, and the Iford road. A detour to the left will bring you into Iford, where the local manor overlooking the Frome is an unforgettable sight.

Cross the road to the gate/stile opposite, and follow the field paths alongside the Frome back towards Farleigh Hungerford. As the castle comes into view, the path forks at a stile (yellow arrows). Either path will lead back to the castle and the neighbouring Hungerford Arms.

15 Midford
The Hope and Anchor

Midford lies deep in a river valley, surrounded by glorious rolling hills and open vistas. Over time, everything has passed this way – footpaths, bridlepaths, the canal and the railway have all left their mark. Today it is the busy B3110, providing a short cut out of Bath for traffic heading south. The Hope and Anchor sits alongside this busy thoroughfare, on a tight bend, dominated by the railway viaduct that once carried the Somerset and Dorset line from Bath to Bournemouth. This is a fine old pub with a lot of character and warmth.

Railway buffs will quickly spot that the Hope and Anchor's car park sits on the old S & D trackbed, sandwiched between the remains of Midford station and Midford viaduct. From the car park, steps lead down past a paved terrace to the inn, naturally fashioned from the local Bath stone. The Hope and Anchor has been the subject of renovation in recent years, but many traditional features remain. These include the wooden floors, the exposed stonework and a number of fine black beams. That most welcoming of sights, a handsome stone fireplace, still remains, and sitting there proudly in the hearth is a genuine anchor. Around the walls hang a good selection of local prints, maps and photographs. The ones that relate to the Somerset and Dorset Railway, an unfortunate victim of the Beeching axe, will perhaps prove of most interest.

The bar menu is chalked up each day in the lounge and offers customers a good range of imaginative dishes. There are such tempting options as chicken paella, traditional Polish bigos and rye bread, pasta provençal, Spanish tortilla salad, and beef, mushroom and Guinness pie. This is in addition to the staple items of ploughman's, soup, steaks and fish dishes. A typical chef's special is rabbit baked with prunes and onions, with a cream and mushroom sauce served with rice, quite a mouthful in more senses than one. It goes without saying that the food at the Hope and Anchor is something out of the ordinary. The beers and ales will prove equally welcome to the discerning palate. With brews such as Smiles, Wadworth 6X, John Smith's Yorkshire Bitter and Butcombe available, there is certainly plenty of choice when it comes to quenching that thirst after your walk.

Telephone: 0225 832296.

How to get there: Midford is on the B3110 Bath to Norton St Philip road, a couple of miles outside Bath. As you drop down the hill into the village, the Hope and Anchor lies on the left-hand side, immediately past the old railway viaduct.

Parking: There is a car park for patrons behind the inn. Other parking opportunities in Midford are very limited. About 100 yards down the main road from the Hope and Anchor, a couple of vehicles could park on the gravelled area on the left-hand side, just before the Limpley Stoke turning. There is also space for a couple of vehicles 100 yards the other side of this turning, on another gravelled area opposite some cottages. Opposite the inn is the Twinhoe road, where a car or two could park tight to the roadside.

Length of the walk: 3 miles. Map: OS Landranger 172 Bristol and Bath (GR 761607).

Midford lies at the junction of a number of valleys that bisect what was the Somerset countryside to the south of Bath. Roads, railways and canals converged on the village from the surrounding valleys, although most are now in a gentle state of decay with nature taking her inevitable course. The remains, however, will fascinate the industrial archaeologist. This walk heads out of Midford on the Twinhoe road, a climb that brings rewarding views over the valley containing Cam Brook. A bridlepath carries us from Upper Twinhoe down to the river, from where the old Somerset Coal Canal is followed back into Midford. On our approaches to the village,

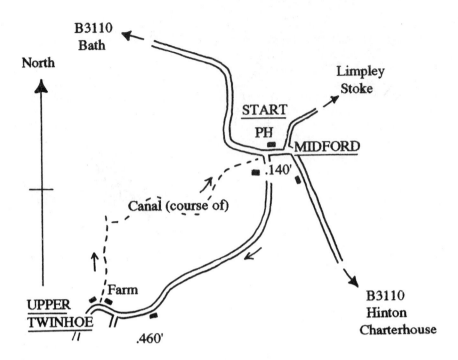

North

B3110
Bath

Limpley
Stoke

START

PH

MIDFORD

.140'

Canal (course of)

Farm

UPPER
TWINHOE

.460'

B3110
Hinton
Charterhouse

Not to scale

the remains of both the Camerton Branch and the Somerset and Dorset Railway remind us of what were the death-knells of the canal, the railways themselves having since fallen victim to road transport.

The Walk

Directly opposite the Hope and Anchor, follow the lane signposted to Twinhoe. This lane initially crosses Cam Brook and passes the point where the Somerset and Dorset Railway crossed the Camerton Branch, before climbing the hillside quite steeply. The OS sheet marks the road with one of those black arrows − gradient 1 in 7 to 1 in 5. The lane eventually levels out and runs across the hilltop, bringing fine views of the valley to the north that our steps back to Midford will follow later. Pass through the tiny hamlet of Middle Twinhoe, 1 mile from Midford, fork right at the first (and only) road junction and continue the short distance on to Upper Twinhoe Farm.

Between the farm buildings and the farmhouse, turn right on to a bridlepath, marked by an insignificant sign on a gatepost. The path descends through open fields initially, before plunging steeply through woodland down to cross Cam Brook. This last section of the bridlepath normally resembles a stream bed! About 30 yards on from the footbridge across the river, cross a stile on the right-hand side into the meadows that run alongside Cam Brook. For the next ½ mile or so, follow the towpath alongside the Somerset Coal Canal. Actually, that is rather stretching a point – it would be better to say, follow the well-worn field path that runs alongside a rather wide ditch, dry in summer months, marshy in the winter. Sharp-eyed walkers may pick out the remains of one or two old lock chambers on the early stages of this towpath stroll.

Eventually, the old canal is literally severed by a vast embankment carrying the old Camerton Branch line – last used, incidentally, in the filming of *The Titchfield Thunderbolt*. The footpath crosses a stile at this point, bears to the right and passes under the viaduct, which carries the old trackbed over Cam Brook. On the other side of the viaduct, the path bears to the left to follow the other side of the embankment to a stile, beyond which you pick up the old canal bed. The path bears to the right, and continues alongside that rather wide ditch. A couple of interesting canal features dominate the next 100 yards. Just past the railway, a perfectly preserved stone over-bridge lies on the left-hand side, whilst a short distance on you will spot an aqueduct crossing Cam Brook. This carried a branch of the canal down to Radstock, the main canal running from the Kennet and Avon at Dundas through to the Somerset Coalfield at Paulton. Continue following the old canal bed across what is now a paddock, to a stile. Beyond this stile, the path enters an area of overgrowth, bordering an unusual garden, before emerging on to the B3110 opposite the Hope and Anchor.

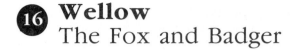

Wellow
The Fox and Badger

Right in the heart of Wellow lies the Fox and Badger inn, a fine stone building whose presence is announced to all and sundry by the magnificent inn sign, depicting a fox and a badger dressed Regency style. Hanging baskets adorn the pub, whilst a pair of bench seats attached to the inn's wall enable visitors to sup their ale whilst taking in the view of Wellow's main street.

Internally, the Fox and Badger exudes a traditional and unspoilt atmosphere. There is a public bar and a lounge, the former blessed with a good collection of old pub games such as table skittles and dominoes. Flagstone flooring, open fireplaces and wooden beams lend a rustic feel to the inn, providing a décor that is complemented by cushioned settles and displays of china, copper and brasses.

A wide-ranging selection of food, listed on large blackboards in the bars, is available at the Fox and Badger. If a light snack is your preference, perhaps smoked mackerel, hot beef sandwiches or a simple Cheddar ploughman's would appeal. Larger appetites are more likely to favour such dishes as pork kebabs, honey-baked ham and fresh pineapple, Cumberland sausage, steaks, steak pie or trout. All the dishes are freshly prepared, well presented, of ample proportions and reasonably priced. If your hunger still persists, a good range of sweets is always available. These might include sorbets, raspberries and cream, lemon cheesecake, or chocolate and almond eclairs. Like any sensible inn nowadays, the Fox and Badger offers a full children's menu. The good selection of food is matched by the excellent beers and ales on offer, for example, Courage Bitter, Butcombe, Wadworth 6X and the marvellous Morland Old Speckled Hen. Superb beers, good food and a delightful village setting make the Fox and Badger a very attractive pub.

Telephone: 0225 832293.

How to get there: The B3110 running south from Bath to Norton St Philip passes through Hinton Charterhouse. Leave the B3110 at this point to follow the unclassified road signposted to Wellow. In just over 2 miles, this road passes beneath the arches of the old Somerset and Dorset Railway viaduct before climbing past St Julian's church into the centre of the village, where the Fox and Badger lies on the left-hand side.

Parking: There is adequate roadside parking in the vicinity of the pub.

Length of the walk: 3 miles. Map: OS Landranger 172 Bristol and Bath (GR 740583).

A hillside village, a ford, a hilltop path, a long barrow and a riverside path, all in peaceful countryside – it is hard to believe we are so close to the city of Bath. The walk has just one or two short steep sections – the climb down to Wellow Brook from the village at the start, the return at journey's end and the climb to Stony Littleton long barrow – but in the main it is level bridlepath, field path and quiet country lane.

The Walk

From the Fox and Badger, follow the road back towards Hinton Charterhouse for a few yards before turning right, just before Wellow village school. This lane drops steeply towards Wellow Brook, passing beneath the severed bridge that once carried the Somerset and Dorset Railway through the village. Just past the old railway bridge, look out for a dwelling on the right-hand side called Tumbledown Cottage. Turn right immediately past this cottage and follow a footpath in front of a rank of terraced cottages, to a stile. Cross the stile, and head straight across the long, thin hay meadow beyond, to a second stile in the far right-hand corner.

A short section of enclosed path continues to an old orchard, now used for grazing cattle. Cross this orchard to another stile, where you

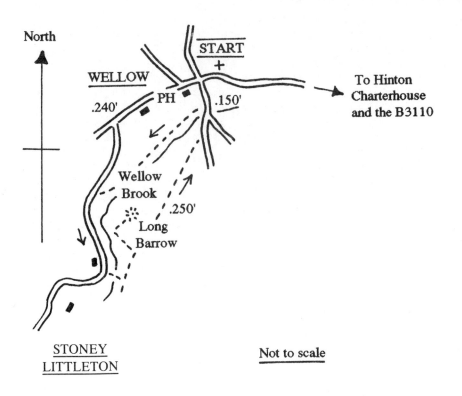

North

START

WELLOW

PH

.240'

.150'

To Hinton
Charterhouse
and the B3110

Wellow
Brook

.250'

Long
Barrow

STONEY
LITTLETON

Not to scale

enter a vast riverside meadow. The aim here is to reach a stile in the far corner – almost ½ mile distant – which brings you on to the Wellow to Stony Littleton lane. The official right of way crosses the middle of the field, but the majority of walkers will prefer to follow the permissive path that borders the banks of Wellow Brook.

Turn left along the lane, which is followed for ½ mile to an isolated cottage called Greenacres – the name is wholly appropriate given its setting amidst the rolling hills of what was formerly north Somerset. Opposite Greenacres, cross the footbridge on the left across Wellow Brook, following a path signposted to Stony Littleton long barrow. Once across the river, the path bears left to a stile, before following the left-hand hedgerow up the hillside. In about 60 yards, a detour is necessary to visit the long barrow itself. A stile on the left-hand side brings you into an open field, where the hedgerow is followed for 150 yards to a stile on the right. Beyond this stile, the path climbs to a fine example of Celtic antiquity. The long barrow is a perfect place to pause at – set on the hillside high above Wellow Brook, with magnificent views across to Wellow, dominated by the tower of the village church, and surrounded by green hills dotted with isolated farms.

Retrace your steps back to the main bridlepath, and turn left to a gate. Beyond this gate, the path crosses a large open field high on the hilltop. Initially the path follows the right-hand hedgerow and, where this ends, it continues in the same direction as an uncultivated strip of what is otherwise an arable field. The path reaches a gate, before continuing for ½ mile as a secluded and enclosed green lane. The hedgerows either side of the path are awash with wild flowers in spring and summer – unfortunately, the path can be awash with mud following heavy rain, due to the presence of a local trekking centre.

The bridlepath eventually joins a quiet lane, where you continue straight ahead for just a few yards to a road junction. Turn left, and the lane descends to Wellow Brook. This is a lovely spot, with a pack-horse bridge alongside a ford, the whole scene overlooked by a most traditionally English cottage. Beyond the ford, continue up the hill back into the centre of Wellow, retracing the route followed at the outset of this circuit.

Nunney
The George

It is difficult to drive through Nunney without being aware of the George. Right across the main street is a rare 'gallows' sign, announcing to all and sundry the location of the village inn. The George fronts on to the High Street, with its whitewashed walls, shutters and window boxes forming part of a handsome exterior. Inside the inn, there is a comfortable and inviting atmosphere. The open-plan bar sits amongst stripped stone walls, with a good supply of tables and chairs, and a fine log fire in winter.

The George offers traditional bar food – sandwiches, rolls, ploughman's and so on – as well as an interesting à la carte menu. The starters include soup, prawn cocktail, home-made pâté and melon, with the main courses being a meat-eater's delight. In addition to the vast steaks, the dishes could include lamb cutlets, venison, Aylesbury duck, poussin or guinea-fowl. As an alternative to meat, perhaps plaice or vegetable au gratin could prove a temptation. Thursday evenings, according to the information board outside the George, see Malaysian fare on offer – although prior booking is advised.

This is a freehouse, with a range of changing real ales available. These could include Butcombe, Webster's Yorkshire Bitter or Exmoor

Ale from Wiveliscombe. In addition, the array of whiskies, brandies and liqueurs presents the connoisseur with an interesting dilemma. Should you not feel up to driving after an hour or two at the inn, there is also accommodation on site.

Telephone: 0373 836458.

How to get there: Nunney lies just 1 mile north of the A361 Shepton Mallet road, 3 miles west of Frome. The George is in the centre of the village.

Parking: The George has a car park for patrons. The Market Place, a few yards along the road from the George, has parking space for a few vehicles. There is also plenty of room for careful roadside parking in the village.

Length of the walk: 2½ miles. Map: OS Landranger 183 Yeovil and Frome (GR 737457).

Nunney is a picturesque village with a surprise at every turn. Behind the main street flows Nunney Brook, home to a vociferous flock of ducks that demand food of every passing visitor. Back in the days of the local cloth industry, the brook provided a 'pavement place to wash wool'. Beyond the river rises the castle, delightfully toy-like in scale, the ruinous condition of which dates back to 1645 and the Civil War. All Saints church is largely a rebuilding, although the chancel dates back to the 13th century. Interspersed amongst these pages from history are a number of dated houses, ranging from 1693 to 1744.

Whilst the village is enough to detain any visitor for an hour or two, the surrounding countryside too provides many a delightful beauty spot. On this walk, the highlight is Nunney Combe, a secluded wooded valley to the north of the village. The footpath follows the banks of Nunney Brook through the combe, where a rich variety of flora and fauna is evident throughout the year. Early spring is my favourite season for this walk, when the river banks are awash with a carpet of white snowdrops.

The Walk

From the George, walk the few yards into the centre of Nunney and turn right on to the signposted Mells road. Cross Nunney Brook and, in just 100 yards, opposite a new house called Flambards, turn right on to an enclosed footpath. This path passes a disused quarry on the left-hand side before emerging into open countryside.

In the first field, follow the right-hand field boundary. The pleasant view to the right looks across Nunney, with the castle taking centre stage. In the next field, continue in the same direction, passing to the left of an isolated tree. The field path descends into a dip before climbing a small embankment into a third field. Aim for the far left-

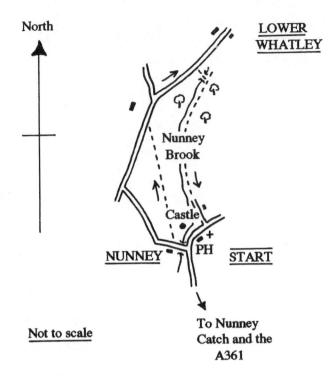

North

LOWER
WHATLEY

Nunney
Brook

Castle

NUNNEY   PH   START

Not to scale

To Nunney
Catch and the
A361

hand corner, where a gateway brings you on to the Mells road.

Turn right and, in just 200 yards, right again on to a quiet lane. In just under ½ mile, in a small dip, follow the gravelled track on the right down to Nunney Brook. You are now in the heart of Nunney Combe, a marvellously secluded valley with the river flowing beneath a canopy of deciduous woodland. Cross the river, and follow the riverside path to the right. In ½ mile, the path leaves the woodland and crosses an open field to reach the driveway leading to Combe Farm. Continue ahead along this driveway until you meet the Frome road on the edge of Nunney. Turn right, and in a few minutes you will find yourself in the heart of the village.

This may be a short walk, but there is so much of interest in Nunney to fill any spare time you may have. The castle is the obvious attraction, but do not overlook All Saints church. The monuments in the north aisle provide a fascinating insight into the changing world of fashion in the 14th, 15th and 16th centuries, whilst the Civil War cannon-ball provides a stark reminder of the reasons for the ruinous state of the castle.

76

18 Nettlebridge
The Nettlebridge Inn

The Foss Way below Radstock sweeps down into the Nettlebridge valley before climbing on towards Beacon Hill, the highest point in East Mendip. In the foot of the valley, alongside the less romantically named A367, lies the Nettlebridge Inn. In the past, the Nettlebridge area was riddled with small-scale coal workings. The local alehouses had a reputation that matched that of the tough mining communities. Today, however, the picture is altogether different, and the handsome, whitewashed Nettlebridge Inn provides a warm welcome to both passing motorists and visitors exploring the locality. The interior has been totally modernised and redecorated, and the atmosphere is relaxed and inviting, with the large lounge/dining area being very much family oriented. Wooden partitions divide up the large lounge into a number of more intimate areas, where a good number of table and chair sets mean that customers rarely have to wait to rest tired limbs. The views from the inn's windows are quite superb. If you arrive early enough, claim the seats alongside the picture window, which provides extensive views eastwards across the Nettlebridge valley and on to Harridge Wood.

The menu on offer at the Nettlebridge Inn covers starters, bar meals, fish, omelettes, salads, jacket potatoes, ploughman's, grills, children's dishes and sweets. A daily selection of specials is also chalked up above the bar. The bar meals include steak and kidney pie, cauliflower cheese, chicken tikka, cottage pie and wings of fire, whilst the grills include rack of ribs, pan-fried steak and trout, served in delicious sauces. The specials are such dishes as home-made 12 inch pizza, herb-coated rack of lamb and beef bourguignonne served on a bed of rice. To ensure an adequate intake of calories, both death by chocolate and apple pie with cream appear on the menu.

The Nettlebridge Inn is owned by the nearby Oakhill Brewery, whose fascinating history appears on the back of the menus. The brewery opened as long ago as the 1780s, and at one time had its own railway line running through to the Somerset and Dorset at Binegar. After run-down and closure, the brewery has once again reopened to supply some quite exceptional beers. Visitors to Nettlebridge will be able to enjoy three Oakhill brews – Strong Ale, Best Bitter and Black Magic.

Telephone: 0749 841360.

How to get there: Nettlebridge lies between Radstock and Shepton Mallet on the A367, 2 miles south of Stratton-on-the-Fosse. As the main road descends into the Nettlebridge valley, the Nettlebridge Inn can be seen on the left-hand side.

Parking: There is a large car park behind the Nettlebridge Inn for patrons. Please ask permission to use the car park.

Length of the walk: 3 miles. Map: OS Landranger 183 Yeovil and Frome (GR 648487).

Nettlebridge sits beside the course of the Foss Way, the ancient Roman highway. This is part of the Eastern Mendips, less spectacular than West Mendip with its gorges, cliffs and caverns, but none the less a fine rural landscape. To the east of Nettlebridge lie Harridge Wood and Stoke Bottom, secluded and lonely wooded valleys, that hide a number of small springs, rock faces and caves. The woodland is also home to a vast range of flora and moisture-loving plants, making this walk a must for the naturalist and the botanist.

The Walk

Leave the inn's car park and turn left, following the pavement alongside the rather busy A367. The road climbs the side of the Nettlebridge valley, with fine sweeping views opening up behind you. Three hundred yards up the hill from the inn, look out for a concrete path on the opposite side of the road. A sign attached to the wall

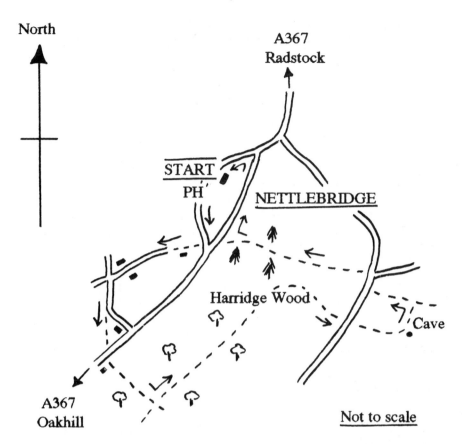

North

A367
Radstock

START
PH

NETTLEBRIDGE

Harridge Wood

Cave

A367
Oakhill

Not to scale

indicates that this path leads to a cottage called 'Bag End'. Cross the road with care, and follow this path up past the cottage. The path soon becomes a country lane which continues past Park Farm and on to a crossroads. Turn left, and follow the turning signposted to Bath.

In 100 yards, by a left-hand bend, cross the stile on the right into a pasture normally occupied by frisky young heifers. Bear left, and cross this field aiming for the main A367 road. As you approach the road, make for the stile in the right-hand corner of the field. Cross the stile and follow the A367 to the right for just a few yards, before crossing another stile on the opposite side of the road. Head straight across this field towards a dip on the far side, to the left of which a stone stile leads into Harridge Wood. Beyond the stile, follow the path ahead downhill to the valley bottom, an old wall bordering the path on the right. At the foot of the slope, you reach a cross track in the heart of this lonely, secluded woodland.

79

Turn left and follow the woodland path for close on ¾ mile. It borders the stream that flows through Harridge Wood, a tributary of the Mells Stream. A number of springs have their source in this valley, and it comes as no surprise to find various water-board installations in this damp habitat. Eventually, the path passes a tumbledown cottage on the left to reach a gateway and the end of the woodland. In the next field, follow the edge of the woods on the right – Limekiln Wood – for 400 yards to a gate that leads on to the Nettlebridge to Doulting lane.

Cross the road, and pass through the gateway opposite. Follow the left-hand hedgerow in the field beyond for 150 yards until you reach a spring on the right-hand side. This is known as St Dunstan's Well, and in the rocks above the spring lies the entrance to a cave with the same name. Alongside the spring, turn left and follow an enclosed path beyond a gateway that runs parallel to a stream. Shortly, you reach a cross track where you turn left along another enclosed path to rejoin the Doulting road.

Turn right, and continue to a road junction. Just past the junction, cross the gate on your left into an open field. The path is not signposted at this point. Cross this field, keeping to the river bank on your left, until the path reaches a stile that leads into Harridge Wood. Follow the path ahead to an old stone bridge, cross the stream and continue up the hill to a woodland clearing. The path bears to the right and continues for close on ½ mile through coniferous plantations before leaving the woodland – an official signpost informs the visitor that this is part of Mendip Forest.

Just past this information board, you join a country lane. This is in fact the route of the Foss Way, running parallel to the adjoining A367. Turn right, and the lane sweeps down the hill through Nettlebridge before rising to join the A367. The straight line of this lane is an obvious clue to the Roman origins of this routeway. Back at the main road, turn left and walk the final few yards back to the Nettlebridge Inn.

⓵⁹ Croscombe
The Bull Terrier

The Bull Terrier, a solid stone-built inn, sits alongside the Wells to Shepton Mallet road in the centre of Croscombe. Dating back to the late 15th century, and first granted a licence to sell alcohol in 1612, the inn was known quite simply as 'The Rose and Crown' until 1976. Not surprisingly, it has more recently become something of a mecca for bull terrier breeders and owners from far and wide.

The inn offers three bar areas, the Inglenook, the Snug and the Common Bar. Cushioned wall seats, wheelback chairs, glossy tables and wooden beams create a traditional atmosphere. This is enhanced by log-effect fires in stone fireplaces in winter, carpeted flagstone floors and a number of pictures, attractively displayed on the white walls. The food on offer is quite outstanding and includes the staples of the pub trade – sandwiches, soup, basket meals, ploughman's and salads – as well as a number of more unusual offerings. These might typically include Indian spiced beans, Brazil nut loaf, Barnsley chop, ginger chicken with noodles and asparagus quiche. A number of tempting sweets could follow your main course, perhaps hot chocolate fudge cake, Bavarian lemon torte or hot butterscotch and walnut fudge cake. Drinkers will be more interested in the Bull

Terrier's fine range of beer and ales. Bull Terrier Best Bitter is specially brewed for the pub, whilst Butcombe, Palmers, Royal Oak and Theakston XB are available on handpump. Service is warm and courteous.

Telephone: 0749 343658.

How to get there: Croscombe lies on the A371, midway between Shepton Mallet and Wells. The Bull Terrier is situated alongside the main road, in the centre of the village.

Parking: There is a limited amount of parking at the Bull Terrier for patrons. Walkers are advised to park carefully in the village. One suggestion is to turn into Church Street, alongside the Bull Terrier. At the top of the hill, bear left into Fayre Way where there is ample room for roadside parking.

Length of the walk: 3 miles. Map: OS Landranger 183 Yeovil and Frome (GR 591444).

Croscombe lies at the head of the Sheppey valley, deep in the folded hills of East Mendip. This walk explores the hillsides to the north and south of the village, in what is a little-known corner of Somerset. Along the way, our steps pass through Ham Woods, awash in springtime with a carpet of traditional English flora. The final return into Croscombe follows one of the most pleasant green lanes in the region. The path meanders down the slopes of the hillside, bounded by classic hedgerows, taking in views of Worminster Down and Knowle Hill on the far side of the valley.

The Walk

From outside the inn, follow the pavement alongside the busy A371 in the direction of Wells, passing the village post office. In just a few yards, turn left into Old Street Lane, before turning right in front of a fine old chapel. The lane continues uphill and out of Croscombe.

At the top of the hill, you will reach a whitewashed cottage on the left-hand side. Turn left on to the bridlepath that runs alongside the cottage, and follow the path across the hillside to a quiet lane, stopping at the gateways on the left to enjoy the superb views of Croscombe, nestled in its steep-sided valley. Turn right at the lane, and continue uphill for a short distance to a road junction high on the hilltop. It is worth crossing to the gateway almost opposite to enjoy an extensive view across the Vale of Avalon, dominated by Glastonbury Tor.

Detour completed, turn left at the junction and follow the hilltop road for just 200 yards until a stile and footpath sign appear at the top of the bank on the left-hand side, just before a road junction. The

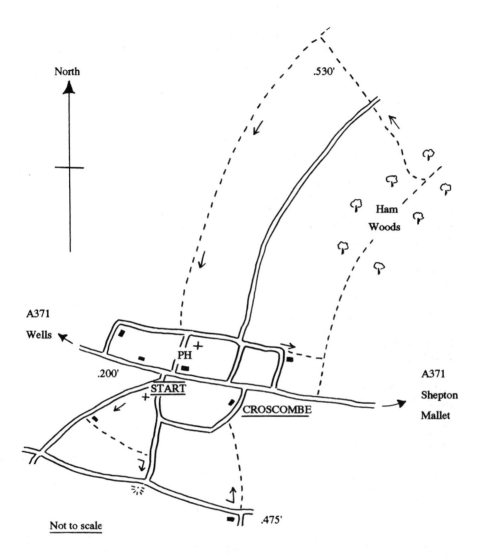

North

.530'

Ham
Woods

A371

Wells

.200'

PH

START

CROSCOMBE

A371

Shepton

Mallet

.475'

Not to scale

footpath is signposted 'Croscombe ¾'.

Climb the steps to the stile, and cross to a gateway in the far left-hand corner of the first field. A quite magnificent view (again) of Croscombe in the valley below opens up. Beyond this gateway, drop straight down the hillside to an enclosed green track below, just to the left of a small enclosure. Continue down this track to a lane, and go across the Sheppey to the A371. Opposite lies the Old Manor.

Turn right along the main road for just a few yards, before turning left into Boards Lane. At the top of the lane, turn right and cross a stile to follow a path signposted 'Ham Wood ¼ mile'. The path follows the edge of a field down to a track, where you turn left to reach a gateway leading into the woods.

Beyond the gateway you enter a delightfully secluded woodland set in a steep-sided valley. Mosses and ferns thrive in this damp habitat, where bare rock exposures line the path. Follow the path along the valley bottom for approximately ½ mile, until the right of way bears to the left and a line of conifers appears ahead, to the right of the footpath. Just before reaching these trees, look out for a boulder on the left bearing a yellow-painted arrow. Follow this footpath to the left, as it leaves the valley bottom to climb the steep valley side.

At the top of this climb, you enter an open field. Cross the field to a gateway, 50 yards to the right of a telegraph pole, and follow the green lane beyond this gateway to a quiet country lane. Turn right and, in a few yards, cross the stile on the left-hand side. A post bears the legend 'Mendip 40 Wells 3 miles'. Follow the right-hand field boundary to join a green lane, where you turn left to go down the hillside. This superb path descends the hillside for ½ mile, back into Croscombe. As you enter the village, the first turning on the right is Fayre Way – where you may well have parked – whilst continuing down the road into Church Street will return you to the inn and the A371.

Glastonbury
The Who'd A Thought It

The Who'd A Thought It sits alongside a narrow, busy stretch of the B3151 Meare Road, just off Glastonbury's High Street. Despite the setting, the inn exudes a cheerful appearance, with its bright whitewashed walls, a number of picnic tables on a side patio, clearly displayed information boards and tubs of flowers. The promotional literature is pleased to announce that, even if you have not found the Holy Grail on your visit to Glastonbury, at least at the Who'd A Thought It you will have discovered a decent pub!

Inside, a warm and friendly welcome awaits all visitors to the inn, housed in what was originally a collection of farm buildings on the edge of the Somerset Levels. Modern developments, however, mean that the Levels are now a mile or so down the road. The bar areas contain a number of original features – black beams, exposed stonework, a fine open fireplace and flagstone flooring – which give the Who'd A Thought It a truly rural feel. The pine tables and chairs complement the inn's décor, and nostalgia is clearly the order of the day. From the well-displayed collections of original china and the traditional metal advertising signs, to the penchant for music from the '20s and '30s, the Who'd A Thought It will please visitors

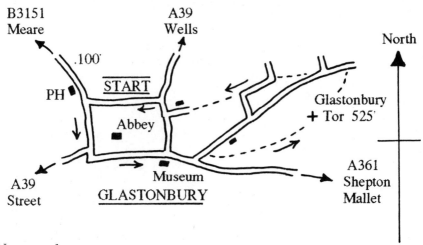

B3151
Meare

A39
Wells

North

.100'

PH

START

Glastonbury
+ Tor 525'

Abbey

A39
Street

Museum
GLASTONBURY

A361
Shepton
Mallet

Not to scale

who talk fondly of the 'good old days'. Visit the pub on a Thursday evening, and chances are you will be blessed with live jazz – of the traditional variety, of course!

There is a good range of well-prepared bar meals, which will readily satisfy the appetites of any hungry walkers. The dishes include lamb chops, curries, vegie hotpot, steak and kidney pie, sirloin steak, kippers and lasagne. One particular option that comes highly recommended is the fruity ploughman's, served with delicious home-made soda bread. As well as this standard bar menu, a range of special dishes is chalked up on blackboards each day. The beers include brews from Bass, Eldridge Pope and Palmers. The latter two are both Dorset brewers – from Dorchester and Bridport respectively – and Eldridge Pope Thomas Hardy Country Bitter is especially recommended. As a final footnote, if you are tempted to stay overnight in the Glastonbury area, then the Who'd A Thought It offers excellent accommodation.

Telephone: 0458 831039.

How to get there: At the western end of the High Street, turn on to the B3151 Meare road. The Who'd A Thought It lies a few yards along this turning on the left-hand side.

Parking: You will find a large public car park in the side street opposite the Who'd A Thought It.

86

Length of the walk: 3 miles. Map: OS Landranger 183 Yeovil and Frome (GR 498390).

The mystical kingdom of Avalon has traditionally been associated with Glastonbury and its famous Tor. In Celtic legend, Avalon was the 'island of the blest' or 'paradise', whilst in Arthurian legend it was the 'land of heroes' to which the dead king was conveyed. Although no longer surrounded by lake and marshland, the massive hillock rising out of the early morning mist as it blankets the Somerset Levels is indeed reminiscent of a mysterious island silhouetted against the Somerset sky.

This short circuit takes you past the Abbey and, steeply, to the top of the Tor, from where the views are superb.

The Walk

Walk along Northload Street back to the end of Glastonbury's High Street, and continue straight ahead along Magdalene Street past the entrance to Glastonbury Abbey. Continue on along Fisher's Hill, past Abbey Park, before turning left into Bere Lane. At the junction with Chilkwell Street, alongside the fine Somerset Rural Life Museum, continue out of town for 400 yards before turning left into Wellhouse Lane.

Just a short distance along Wellhouse Lane, turn right to follow the signposted footpath to the Tor. Follow the obvious route to the hilltop, where you will undoubtedly pause to enjoy one of the finest views in Somerset. A convenient topograph highlights the many landmarks. Follow the steps down the eastern side of the Tor to reach the northern end of Wellhouse Lane.

Turn left at the road and, in 400 yards, look out for a stile on the right-hand side, just past a road junction. Cross this stile and bear half-left to reach a second clearly visible stile. Follow the right-hand hedgerow beyond this stile, to Lypyatt Lane.

Ahead, the lane bears sharply to the left. At this point, continue straight ahead on a footpath that descends Chalice Hill. A conveniently placed bench will enable you to enjoy the views across Glastonbury to the Levels and beyond. The footpath joins Dod Lane, which leads down to Chilkwell Street. Turn right and, in 200 yards, left into Glastonbury's High Street. Walk down the High Street, with its many New Age emporia, before turning right into Northload Street to reach the Who'd A Thought It.

Wookey Hole
The Wookey Hole Inn

Wookey Hole Caves are one of Mendip's great tourist attractions. Vast caverns carved out of the limestone hills by the subterranean river Axe. The Wookey Hole Inn, a substantial stone and whitewash building, stands opposite the entrance to the caves complex. The inn sign, a silhouette of a witch, is a reminder of just one of the ghostly figures that allegedly lie deep under the hills. In truth, the Witch of Wookey is none other than a stalagmite formation, but the legend suggests that this pair of stalagmites are the petrified remains of a witch and her dog, turned to stone when a monk doused them with holy water.

The Wookey Hole Inn literally fronts on to the busy access road to the caves. Step inside, however, and you will find a bright and airy atmosphere that is welcoming and comfortable. The white and turquoise colour scheme in the bar areas is most attractive, extending beyond the wood panelling and walls to the cushioned pew seats and bar stools. With matching carpets, pine table and chair sets, a marbled fireplace and baskets of dried flowers, it is obvious that a lot of care and attention has gone into the décor of this inn. Around the walls is displayed a selection of local black and white photographs, including the village bowling team in action, the river Axe and Mendip strawberry growing. On warm summer days, patrons can enjoy their refreshment seated in the most attractive rear garden, a peaceful respite from the crowds visiting the nearby caves.

The bar menu offers customers starters, ploughman's, salads, sandwiches, main courses, vegetarian dishes, jacket potatoes and children's dishes. Vegetarians will surely be tempted by the cashew and mixed nut paella, whilst meat-eaters might favour the home-made steak and kidney pie, or the chicken Kiev. Youngsters will, of course, be pleased to see trusty favourites such as chicken nuggets, sausages and fish fingers, appropriately served with baked beans and chips. Each day, a number of special dishes, such as pizza or beef curry, are displayed on a board. Death by chocolate is a notable sweet.

The climb on to the Mendip hilltops above Wookey will certainly incite a thirst in even the most hardened of walkers. Fortunately, a number of good beers are available at the Wookey Hole Inn. These include Ushers Best, Founders and Triple Crown, together with Beamish Stout. As we are in Somerset, a local West Country cider is quite rightly available too.

Telephone: 0749 672236.

How to get there: Wookey Hole is well signposted from the nearby city of Wells. The village actually lies on the unclassified road from Wells to Priddy. As you enter Wookey Hole from Wells, the Wookey Hole Inn is on the right-hand side, just before the entrance to the caves.

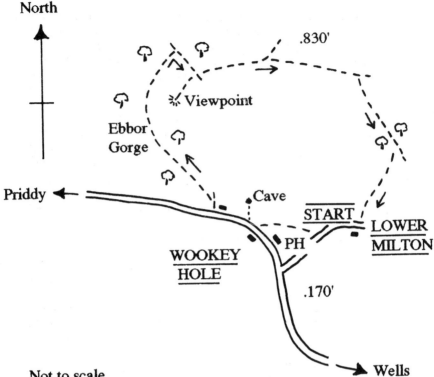

North

.830'

Viewpoint

Ebbor
Gorge

Priddy ←

Cave

START

LOWER
MILTON

WOOKEY
HOLE

PH

.170'

Not to scale

Wells
via A371

Parking: There is a car park for patrons, opposite the inn, as well as room for careful roadside parking between the inn and the village church.

Length of the walk: 4 miles. Map: OS Landranger 182 Weston-super-Mare and Bridgwater (GR 533476).

Wookey Hole village, with its fine showcaves, is one of the great attractions of Mendip. Any feelings of claustrophobia, however, will soon disappear as you climb over 700 ft to the bare and open hilltops that tower above the village. What makes this climb particularly exciting is the rocky scramble that the path takes up through Ebbor Gorge. This dry Mendip valley, with small caves that once sheltered wolves, bears and ancient man, is not for the faint-hearted! The views from the hilltops reach deep into the Somerset Levels, although the eye will inevitably focus upon Glastonbury Tor, the very heart of Avalon.

90

The Walk

From the Wookey Hole Inn, follow the road past the entrance to the showcaves and on to the edge of the village. Alongside Elm Batch, the last residence in Wookey Hole, turn right through the gateway where a marker-post indicates that Priddy is 3 miles away. Very shortly, the path bears to the left to pass through a delightful wooded valley. In just ¼ mile, you will reach a stile at the entrance to the Ebbor Gorge Nature Reserve.

Continue along the path through the reserve until, in a few hundred yards, you take the second of two adjoining turnings on the right-hand side. It is signposted to 'The Gorge'. After a steep, rocky climb of several hundred feet, the path reaches a junction at the hilltop where you turn right. Shortly, another junction is reached where you turn left to continue the climb out of Ebbor Nature Reserve.

It is worth turning right at this second junction to reach a viewpoint overlooking the gorge, before retracing your steps.

Continue the climb out of Ebbor Gorge, crossing a gate/stile and continuing to a second gate/stile, alongside which is an information board. Beyond this second stile, carry on ahead keeping the fence on your left-hand side. When you reach a gateway, bear right and follow the field boundary across the hilltop – do not pass through the gateway. Continue heading eastwards across the hilltop, keeping the field boundary to your left, through several fields. The views to the south (your right) are quite magnificent, stretching across the Somerset Levels to the Quantocks, the Blackdown Hills and Exmoor.

After one final gateway, you emerge into an open field. Bear half-right, dropping down the hillside, to a gate in the right-hand hedgerow. Beyond this gate, the enclosed path continues downhill for 300 yards before passing through a small area of woodland and out into an open field. The path carries on as a grassy track, initially following the right-hand field boundary, to yet another gateway, and then on downhill to the lane at Lower Milton.

Turn right, and continue downhill until you reach Myrtle Farm (*circa* 1689) on the right-hand side. Just past the farm outbuildings, climb the steps to a stile, and follow a path indicating that Wookey Hole is but ¼ mile away. The path heads across a couple of fields back to Wookey Hole village, the distant houses acting as a landmark. In the left-hand corner of the second field, a stile brings you on to a path that leads down to the Priddy road in Wookey Hole. Turn left, and the Wookey Hole Inn is just a few yards along the road.

Litton
The King's Arms

Litton is a picturesque village that lies between Chewton Mendip and West Harptree, surrounded by the gentle hills of East Mendip. The King's Arms, a whitewashed 15th century inn, lies at the bottom of a small valley beside the banks of the infant river Chew. The setting is quite delightful. The terraced gardens that slope down to the river's edge are blessed with a number of picnic tables which enable visitors to fully enjoy the inn's beautiful setting.

Internally, the King's Arms is like a page from a history book – low ceilings, dark-wood beams, flagstone flooring, exposed stonework and vast stone fireplaces are everywhere. The inn's furnishings complement this historic atmosphere. Dark-wood tables, barrel seats, high-backed wooden settles and cushioned window seats are found throughout, and many traditional artefacts are on view. These include brasses, copper pots, china and various agricultural implements, as well as a full suit of armour and a number of heraldic shields. The prints displayed around the walls add a further element of interest for visitors awaiting the inn's quite excellent cuisine.

The menu adopts a courtly theme, in keeping with the name displayed on the inn sign, 'Ye Olde Kings Arms'. Starters, for example, are listed on the menu under the heading 'To start the reign', whilst other sections of the menu include 'The Courtiers' Platters', 'From the Royal Line', 'From the Dragon's Lair', 'Fit for a King' and 'Litton's Lyte Bytes'. It would be impossible to do justice to the imaginative food in just a few lines, such is its scope and diversity. Suffice to say, however, that in a menu that ranges from cheese sandwiches through pigman's platter or lamb cutlets to Japanese prawn or swordfish, there is something for everybody. To accompany your meal, a number of fine beers are available, including Courage Bitter, Wadworth 6X, Bass and Butcombe Bitter.

The King's Arms is rapidly becoming one of the most popular hostelries in the area, and it is not difficult to see why. The setting is idyllic, the interior of the inn delightfully traditional, the atmosphere welcoming, and the menu excellent.

Telephone: 0761 241301.

How to get there: Litton lies on the B3114, between Chewton Mendip and West Harptree, and west of Midsomer Norton. As you drive though the village, the King's Arms is alongside the main road.

Parking: There is a large car park for patrons by the King's Arms. Walkers may prefer to park in the village initially. Driving through Litton from Chewton Mendip, turn right just past the King's Arms on to a quiet lane that leads into the heart of the village. Follow this lane around to the village hall, where there is room for careful roadside parking.

Length of the walk: 3 miles. Map: OS Landranger 182 Weston-super-Mare and Bridgwater (GR 594546).

Litton lies on the fringes of East Mendip, a landscape characterised by gentle hills and lush valleys. To the north of the village, hidden away by folds in the hills, lie two secluded reservoirs formed by damming the river Chew. This circuit explores both the village of Litton and its neighbouring reservoirs, as well as the open expanses of Shortwood Common with its fine views across the area. A delightful walk in a little-explored corner of the north of Somerset.

The Walk

Although there is a car park at the King's Arms, in consideration to patrons it is best to park on the roadside in the vicinity of Litton village hall. Follow the signposted footpath alongside the hall across three fields, keeping to the left-hand hedgerows that border the infant river Chew. This path soon emerges on to the lane running from Litton to Hinton Blewett.

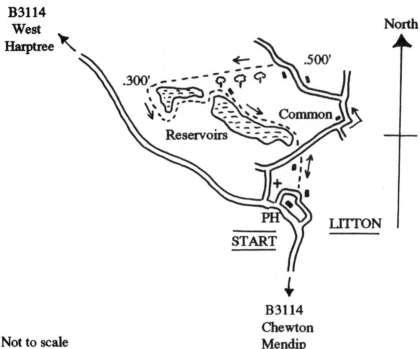

B3114
West
Harptree

North

.300'

.500'

Common

Reservoirs

PH

START

LITTON

Not to scale

B3114
Chewton
Mendip

Turn right, and follow this quiet byway for ½ mile as it passes Elm Tree Farm, before bearing left beyond an isolated cottage. A little further along, the lane forks. Bear left on to a delightful unenclosed lane that climbs up across Shortwood Common. The views that open up are far ranging, stretching back across the village of Litton and beyond, as far as the aerial on Pen Hill above Wells. The road passes Shortwood Farm on the right before bearing left behind Shortwood House.

About 100 yards beyond Shortwood House, the lane bears sharply to the right. At this point, pass through the gateway directly in front of you, and walk down a muddy track for just a few yards to a second gateway. In the next field, bear half-right and walk downhill, aiming for the corner of the woodland on the left. The woods bear the delightful name of Peak's Girt Wood. Continue downhill, alongside the far side of this woodland, with the right of way crossing the field some 20 yards to the right of the trees. At the far end of this hillside pasture, you will find a stile in the hedgerow beneath a fine old oak tree. In the field beyond, aim for the far left-hand corner and a stile that brings you out alongside the dam at the foot of Litton Lower Reservoir.

The next mile or so of walking follows the banks of Litton's Lower and Upper Reservoirs, and delightful walking it is too. The banks are awash with flora in springtime – primroses, bluebells, wood anemone, violets, campion – whilst the reservoirs themselves are home to a rich variety of wildfowl, including moorhen, coot, mallard, swan and the tufted duck. The netted section of water immediately below the upper dam, incidentally, is where fish breeding takes place. You will quickly spot fish surfacing as you look down on this part of the reservoir complex.

Cross the dam in front of you and bear right across the overflow bridge. Immediately past this bridge, turn left along a signposted path into open fields. Follow the left-hand field boundaries across the next pair of fields, the reservoir lying the other side of the hedgerows, and continue along the far side of the second field until you reach a footbridge on the left-hand side. Cross this bridge, and follow the path on the left that follows the banks of a stream running down to the Lower Reservoir. Continue along the banks of the reservoir, cross the upper dam, and follow the path alongside the Upper Reservoir as it passes in front of a cottage.

About ½ mile on from this cottage, the path leaves the reservoir and joins the Litton to Hinton Blewett byway. It is now a simple matter of retracing the route followed at the outset. Look out for the stile across the road that takes you back into those three fields followed on the outward leg of the walk, and follow the hedgerows alongside the Chew back to Litton village hall and the King's Arms.

 Cheddar
The King's Head

The King's Head is a little way from the centre of the village, lying off the normal tourist trail, and is a traditional pub with a relaxed feel and atmosphere. This is a fine old building, with its whitewashed walls and thatched roof, hanging baskets and attractive flower beds complementing the inn's handsome appearance. The entrance to the King's Head leads into a paved courtyard, where a number of local black and white photographs catch the eye. To the right lie the two bars, and passing through the courtyard brings you to the attractive rear garden. A well-stocked aviary adds an element of interest, whilst the views from the picnic tables extend to the hills either side of Cheddar Gorge. The bar areas are cosy and welcoming, with well-restored stone, white plaster and a good number of black beams. Large inglenook fireplaces reveal the age of the King's Arms, with copper bed-warmers, cider pots and bellows decorating the surrounds. The comfortable furnishings consist of carpeted floors, dark-wood tables, cushioned seats and stools.

The menu is divided into starters, omelettes, fish dishes, ploughman's, hot and cold dishes, sandwiches, jacket potatoes, sweets and children's dishes. Amongst the hot dishes, caveman's grill, home-made pie of the day or honey roast chicken would satisfy the most voracious of appetites, whilst fisherman's platter from the fish selections presents patrons with a good mix of seafood delicacies. Traditional appetites will welcome the sweet menu, where sponge pudding, fruit flan and apple pie are to be found – all home-made and served with custard. Good beers and ales are also available at the King's Head. These might, typically, include Ushers Best and Triple Crown, as well as Courage Best.

The King's Head is a lovely old pub, full of comfortable tradition. A most welcome hostelry at the end of a demanding Mendip ramble. Telephone: 0934 742153.

How to get there: The King's Head is not the easiest pub to find. Leave the A371 Weston to Wells road in Cheddar village, and follow the B3135 northwards towards Cheddar Gorge. In ¼ mile, turn into Birch Hill, an unclassified road on the left-hand side that runs between a newsagent's and a chip shop. At the top of Birch Hill, the road bears left into Silver Street. The King's Head lies 400 yards along Silver Street on the right-hand side.

Parking: There is a car park for patrons, alongside the King's Head, whilst there is ample room for roadside parking near the inn.

Length of the walk: 4½ miles. Map: OS Landranger 182 Weston-super-Mare and Bridgwater (GR 457539).

This walk follows paths atop the cliffs on both sides of the gorge, high above the noise and fumes of the road. The views are quite superb and the physical landscape is perhaps the most dramatic in Southern England. Incidentally, the clifftop paths are unfenced and run alongside 450 ft vertical drops – please take great care. The steep gradients on this energetic route reward you with spectacular scenery.

The Walk
Walk back along Silver Street to the point where it bears right to head down Birch Hill into Cheddar. Rather than continue down Birch Hill, turn left into a cul-de-sac lane, which begins to climb uphill out of Cheddar. In just 200 yards, turn right on to a track that leaves the lane just before Rockland House. In 100 yards, just past a chalet bungalow on the left, the path forks. Bear left to begin the long haul up the western side of the gorge.

The path climbs steadily for the next ½ mile, the main consolation being the welcome shelter provided by the bushes and trees that line the path – hawthorn, gorse, hazel and bramble. En route, the path passes through a wall via a handgate, before climbing to a second wall

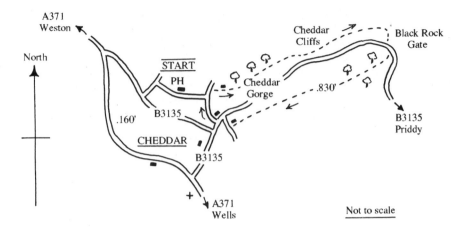

and a stile. The next few steps are vital. Cross the stile, but, rather than follow the path ahead, walk around the corner of the wall and follow its far side out on to open scrubland. You have now left the official right of way as shown on the OS map, to enter a National Trust property known as Cheddar Cliffs, on the western side of the gorge.

Follow the path across this scrubland, as it bears to the left to continue uphill, running parallel to a stone wall. In a short distance, a marker post offers two options. A right turn is signposted to 'The View'. This is a cul-de-sac path that leads to a viewpoint, high above the road, which is both spectacular and dramatic. Having taken this almost mandatory diversion, return to the path and follow the second option on uphill towards Black Rock. In 350 yards, the path passes through a handgate/stile at the end of a wall, before continuing across the edge of the hilltop towards Black Rock. The views across the gorge and the surrounding hillsides are quite superb. This level path eventually descends quite steeply, bears to the right and joins the B3135 at the top of Cheddar Gorge. Turn left, and follow the road for a short distance to the Black Rock Gate parking area.

On the right-hand side, cross a stile that brings you to a footpath leading into thick woodland. A sharp ascent through the trees brings you to the high ground at the top end of Cheddar Gorge. Once you reach the open ground above the woodland, follow the well-worn path that heads back to Cheddar. Shortly, there is a left-hand fork to Draycott, which you ignore, beyond which the path follows the clifftop, many hundreds of feet above the road. Across the gorge, the path that was followed across Cheddar Cliffs can be seen. The scenery is sublime, and almost defies description. It is certainly worth pointing out the danger facing you if you decide to creep too close to the cliff edge to view what appear to be toy cars struggling up the road far below!

Eventually, the path reaches the observation tower at the top of Jacob's Ladder back in Cheddar. Follow the footpath to the left of the tower. This soon joins a lane. Turn right and walk back into the heart of Cheddar. When you reach the B3135, turn left and cross the river. There on the right you will find the chip shop, the newsagent's and Birch Hill. Follow Birch Hill up to Silver Street, turn left and you will shortly arrive back at the King's Head.

East Brent
The Knoll Inn.

The village of East Brent lies in the shadow of Brent Knoll, a strange islanded hill that dominates the western edges of Somerset's central plain. Legend has it that when the devil was carving out nearby Cheddar Gorge he threw a handful of soil across this corner of Somerset, and it fell to form the knoll. With the view from the front of the inn looking directly across to Brent Knoll, the name of this hostelry comes as no surprise.

The Knoll, with its whitewashed walls and attractive hanging baskets, is a traditional local pub. To the right of the off-sales window lies the comfortable lounge bar, whilst across the way is the more basic public bar. The tiled floor, the juke box and the dartboard suggest that this is where serious pub business takes place. The lounge is carpeted, and comfortably furnished with a good number of wooden table and chair sets. Wood panelling extends halfway up the walls, as well as adorning the bar itself, whilst a number of black beams support the ceiling. Around the walls hang brass and copper artefacts, together with a number of old black and white photographs of life in East Brent in years past. An item that caught my eye was a 1900 handbill advertising an outing to Plymouth for the local Society of Oddfellows. The fare was 5/6d return, the train calling at the long-gone Brent Knoll station.

A conventional range of pub food is available at the Knoll Inn, listed on the menu under four main headings – starters, main meals, snacks and sweets. The main meals include chicken, gammon, roast beef, cod, faggots or sausages, whilst the snacks are ploughman's, rolls, sandwiches, jacket potatoes and toasted sandwiches. Each day, a range of specials, perhaps rump and fillet steaks, goujons of plaice or lasagne, is displayed on a board. The portions are ample, well prepared and represent value for money, the type of nourishment needed before or after a strenuous walk up Brent Knoll. This is a Whitbread pub, which means that beers such as Whitbread Bitter, Trophy and West Country Pale Ale are available, together with Flowers Original. Other good beers on offer include Bass and Boddingtons.

Telephone: 0278 760335.

How to get there: East Brent lies on the A370, which links Weston-super-Mare with the A38, 3 miles north of Highbridge. On reaching the village, a right turn into Brent Road leads you to the inn, on the left.

Parking: There are parking spaces in front of the Knoll Inn for patrons. Careful roadside parking is also possible in the vicinity of the inn. To avoid a section of road walking which has to be repeated at the end of the walk, you may prefer to park outside St Mary's in East Brent, and do the circular walk based upon the church.

Length of the walk: 3 miles from the Knoll Inn, or 2 miles from St Mary's church. Map: OS Landranger 182 Weston-super-Mare and Bridgwater (GR 350519 if you start at the pub, 344519 if you start at the church).

Akin to Glastonbury Tor, some miles to the east, Brent Knoll towers over the surrounding Levels, a lonely outpost of the underlying rock formation. This walk is simply an excursion to the summit of Brent Knoll, which provides one of the most expansive views in the area. The hilltop also carries the extensive remains of an ancient hill fort. Back in East Brent, St Mary's church will repay careful exploration. Where else but in Somerset would you find a stained-glass window with natural history and cricket as its themes?

The Walk

From the Knoll Inn, walk back to the A370, cross over and continue along Brent Road as far as the butcher's shop on the left-hand side. Just

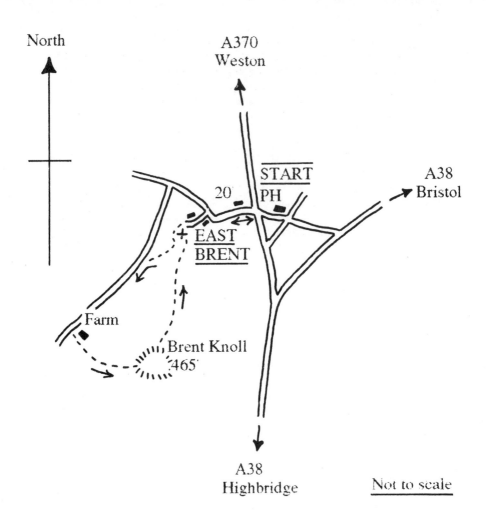

North

A370
Weston

START
PH

20

A38
Bristol

+ EAST
BRENT

Farm

Brent Knoll
465'

A38
Highbridge

Not to scale

past this shop, turn left into a street signposted as leading to the church. Follow the footpath to the right of the church, ignoring the signposted left turn to the Knoll itself. At the top of the churchyard, turn left and follow the path to a gate in the corner of the burial area.

Beyond this gate, bear half-right across the field to a stile in the opposite hedgerow. Cross the stile, and bear half-right to reach another stile in the top corner of the field. This brings you on to the East Brent to Brent Knoll lane. Turn left, and continue along this quiet byway for ½ mile, until you reach Manor Farm. This section of road walking brings a fine view of the Knoll, whilst looking back over your shoulder you will find a panoramic view of the Mendip Hills.

102

Turn left at the farm, pass the house and outbuildings and continue to an open field. Cross to the gateway in the top left-hand corner of this field, and then follow the right-hand hedgerow beyond as it climbs the western slopes of Brent Knoll. A stile at the top of the field brings you to a few steps that quickly secure the hilltop. The views from the Knoll are quite superb: Glastonbury Tor, the Bristol Channel, Exmoor, the Quantocks, the Mendips, the Somerset Levels – the list of landmarks is virtually endless.

Follow the hilltop fortifications around to a flagpole at the northern end of the Knoll. At this point a steep path descends the hillside for over 100 yards to reach a stile. Beyond this stile, keep walking in the direction of East Brent church. The field paths are well used, and a steady succession of waymarked stiles indicate the route. The path eventually passes through the school playground, before reaching the church. It is now a simple question of retracing your steps to the Knoll Inn – or driving if you initially parked at the church.

Cross
The White Hart

Cross is a straggling village that lies beneath the southern slopes of some of the most attractive countryside in West Mendip. High above the village towers Wavering Down, a beautiful area of limestone grassland now owned by the National Trust, whilst away to the south stretch the Somerset Levels. The White Hart fronts on to the main road through the village, the Old Coach Road, today a quiet byway thanks to the construction of the A38 and the M5 motorway. In centuries past, however, the inn would have echoed to the voices of travellers making the arduous journey between London and North Devon. It is a handsome building, with whitewashed walls and a colourful inn sign that make it a prominent landmark along the Old Coach Road. Given the inn's age, it is not surprising to find an abundance of exposed stonework and dark beams inside. The lounge is comfortably furnished with oak table and chair sets, whilst around the walls hangs a collection of horse brasses and prints. The public bar is simply furnished, with a pool table and numerous bar stools suggesting that this is where the locals congregate.

A good variety of dishes is displayed on the blackboard in the White Hart, wholesome portions of well-prepared pub food at reasonable prices. Starters might include soup, prawn cocktail, cheese and ham crêpe or breaded mushrooms and garlic dip, whilst the main courses include steak, chicken and fish dishes, steak and kidney pie, ploughman's, sandwiches, toasties and jacket potatoes. The lemon sole stuffed with crab meat is a particularly tempting option, as is the chicken and Brie. An interesting selection of sweets is also on offer, including chocolate fudge cake, apricot and peach pie, Orlando lemon cheesecake and something called 'humpy pumpy'. Ushers, the Trowbridge-based brewery, controls the White Hart. This means that fine beers such as Ushers Triple Crown, Founders and Best Bitter are available, together with Courage Best and John Smith's.

The White Hart is everything an English inn should be. It offers good beers, traditional pub food and comfortable surroundings. It has been spared the ravages of too much modernity and offers the visitor a warm welcome in hospitable surroundings. The only disappointment was my failure to meet the ghost. After Judge Jeffreys carried out his bloody assizes in the late 17th century, one local victim allegedly returned to haunt the White Hart, so be warned when returning to your car on those dark winter evenings!

Telephone: 0934 732260.

How to get there: Cross lies just to the west of the A38, 15 miles south of Bristol. Turn alongside the New Inn, which is situated on the main A38, on to the Old Coach Road. The White Hart is 200 yards along this quiet lane, on the right-hand side.

Parking: There is a car park for patrons, opposite the White Hart. Roadside parking is also possible in the vicinity of the inn.

Length of the walk: 5 miles. Map: OS Landranger 182 Weston-super-Mare and Bridgwater (GR 418548).

This relatively strenuous excursion is a walk of great contrasts, with the Cheddar Yeo draining the northern margins of the Somerset Levels in the shadow of the Mendip uplands. On the hills, Wavering Down's limestone grassland provides a habitat that attracts migrant ring ouzels and wheatears, as well as stonechats and the now rare dotterel, while the nearby summit of Crook Peak is an exceptional viewpoint. The Bristol Channel, Glastonbury Tor and Brent Knoll are but the more obvious landmarks.

The Walk

From the White Hart continue westwards through the village of Cross for ¼ mile to a left turn, signposted to Weare and Highbridge. Turn left, and continue for 200 yards to Bow Bridge and the Cheddar Yeo.

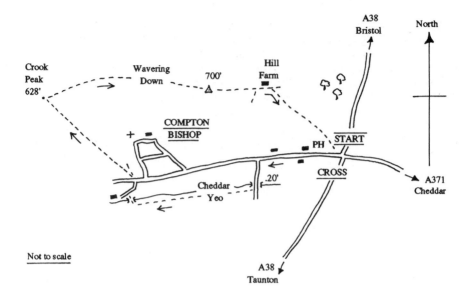

Not to scale

Once over the river, cross the stile on the right and follow the field path that runs alongside the Yeo. Continue along the river bank for 1 mile, following a level path, with the Somerset Levels away to the south. To the north, Crook Peak, Wavering Down and West Mendip dominate the landscape, a reminder that some climbing lies just around the corner.

When you reach a stone bridge, just 400 yards on from a slender footbridge, cross the Yeo and follow the gravelled track ahead for 100 yards to a lane. Turn right to reach the Cross to Loxton road. At the road junction, follow the signposted footpath opposite. In just a few yards, the path forks. Bear left and follow the permissive path that follows the ridge to Crook Peak – a climb of something like 560 ft in just 1 mile. The views from the summit are superb – if you have picked a clear day. Old Admiralty charts mark the peak as 'see me not', an indication of its unreliability as a landmark for coastal shipping. This can be put down to the fact that low cloud very often envelops the rocky outcrops at the summit.

From Crook Peak, head east (to the right) and follow a wide, grassy path that initially descends to what, in the mountains, would be termed a col. Beyond this depression, the path climbs to Compton Hill and Wavering Down, crossing a fine area of limestone grassland. The stone wall on your left, incidentally, follows the Avon/Somerset boundary.

After a stiff climb, you will reach the trig point high on Wavering

106

Down. Another fine view opens up, especially to the south, across the Somerset Levels towards Glastonbury Tor. Having regained your breath, continue along the hilltop path as it descends towards Hill Farm. In front of the farmhouse, bear right to follow another permissive path, across a prominent ridge, labelled on the OS sheet as 'Cross Plain'. Be careful not to take a slightly earlier path that almost immediately descends the hillside back into Cross. In ½ mile, descend the far side of the ridge to reach a handgate, beyond which an enclosed path brings you back into Cross. At the road, turn right and follow the Old Coach Road the short distance back to the White Hart.

26 Rowberrow
The Swan

Rowberrow has not always been the picture of rural tranquillity that is presented to today's visitor. In the 19th century, extracting calamine was the main local employment. It was said that a lawless band of men earned their living in this way, and undoubtedly the local hostelries were far less welcoming places than inns like the Swan are today.

The Swan sits on the hillside, ¼ mile up the road from St Michael's church. If the weather is kind, the garden in front of the inn brings fine views back towards Dolebury Fort. This is an excellent spot for refreshment after the strenuous walk across the hills from Burrington. If the Mendips are running to form, however, you will probably seek shelter from the elements inside. What you will find is a very traditional inn, with a welcoming atmosphere for locals and visitors alike. Internally, there are two main bar areas, both furnished in a tasteful and comfortable manner. The flagstone floors have largely been hidden beneath carpeting, but a number of original features remain. These include an abundance of black beams and some exposed stonework. A selection of interesting prints is displayed around the walls, including one of a group of foxes sitting at a banqueting table enjoying a veritable feast, whilst from the beams hang an array of iron and copper artefacts. A good number of dark-wood tables and chairs are provided for customers, together with cushioned window seats.

The bar menu at the Swan offers standard pub fare, with the dishes on offer including soup, salads, pizza, jacket potatoes, sandwiches, ploughman's and pâté. If the walk across the hills has left you in need of a hot meal, then perhaps a curry or chilli con carne would be tempting. The dishes are well presented and substantial, the beef salad, for example, not only containing a large quantity of beef but also being served with an excellent selection of pickles and chutney. A small number of sweets are available, including those faithful standbys apple pie and ice cream. The beers available at the Swan include Butcombe Bitter, Wadworth 6X and Bass, whilst a guest beer is usually on offer.

Telephone: 0934 852371.

How to get there: Rowberrow is off the A38 just south of Churchill on the way to Axbridge. The Swan is ¼ mile uphill from St Michael's church.

Parking: There is plenty of parking in a car park in front of the pub. Ask permission before parking.

Length of the walk: 6 miles. Map: OS Landranger 182 Weston-super-Mare and Bridgwater (GR 451583).

An energetic walk on the Mendip Hills. The scenery throughout is magnificent, and includes the limestone cliffs and pot-holes of Burrington, the extensive views from the ramparts of the hill fort at Dolebury, the wooded slopes of Rowberrow Bottom that belie the area's former status as a mining centre, and the bracken-and-heather-clad slopes of Blackdown. This walk is best tackled when a ridge of high pressure is firmly settled over southern England, for Mendip is renowned locally for her wet and windy climate.

The Walk
Turn left out of the Swan and follow School Lane down to Rowberrow Bottom. A delightful woodland walk follows for the next ½ mile, with the path bordering a stream alongside the Forestry Commission plantation. Eventually, you will reach a clearing in the woods, and a Water Board installation. Here you follow the track which slopes back up the hill on your left-hand side, signposted to Blackdown. As you climb up through the woods, there are several paths that fork off to both the left and the right. Provided that you follow the main path, through rows of pine trees, straight ahead and

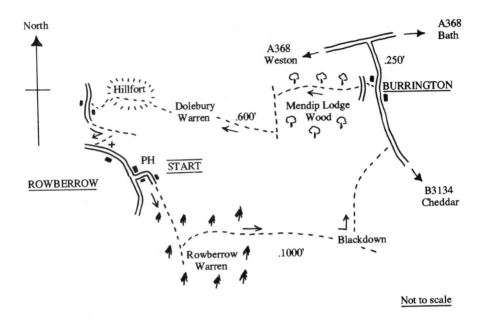

North

A368
Bath

A368
Weston

.250'

BURRINGTON

Hillfort

Dolebury
Warren   .600'

Mendip Lodge
Wood

B3134
Cheddar

PH   START

ROWBERROW

Blackdown

Rowberrow
Warren   .1000'

Not to scale

always climbing, you will not lose your way.

In just under 1 mile, you emerge on to the open hilltop of Blackdown. The highest ground on Mendip is old red sandstone, very different to the limestone found in the valleys. The change in geology as you emerge on to Blackdown is marked by a change in vegetation, with bracken and heather covering the hillside. The path continues straight ahead. Follow the higher right-hand ride, climbing steadily towards the triangulation pillar at Beacon Batch. Cross a wide ride ¼ mile ahead, and continue to a second path on the left, which heads down the hillside to Burrington.

The path down the hillside follows the western side of the shallow valley containing West Twin Brook. Towards the bottom of the hillside, ½ mile further on, take the first small path on the right that drops down into the wooded valley below. Once into this wooded valley, a pebble-strewn path is followed down to the B3134 road. This path is the bed of West Twin Brook, and the amount of surface water will depend upon recent rainfall. A footpath in the trees bordering the road is followed down to the Rock of Ages with a car park opposite, passing en route Aveline's Hole, a limestone cavern.

The Rock of Ages was immortalised in Toplady's splendid hymn, which gave its name to the famous landmark. Walk down the road, past the Burrington Freehouse, until you reach the originally named 'Cottage' on the left-hand side. Climb the steep enclosed path to its left until it joins a quiet lane. Turn left and continue along this lane for just 100 yards to a footpath on the right-hand side. Follow this footpath through Mendip Lodge Wood for ¾ mile until you reach a clearing and the ruinous remains of a group of buildings. The path forks at this point. Bear right and continue for a short distance to a prominent cross-track. Turn left, and follow this track through the trees for 400 yards until you reach the entrance, on the right-hand side, into the National Trust's Dolebury Fort.

Take the well-used path across the open field, and then cross the stile on the right-hand side into the wooded plantation. Bear left, and ½ mile of fine ridge walking follows to bring you to the hill fort, the finest on Mendip and some 20 acres in area. On a clear day, this is a spot you will be very reluctant to leave. The views are immense. Northwards lies Chew Valley, to the west is Weston-super-Mare and the Bristol Channel, Crook Peak is prominent to the south-west, whilst the upland mass of Blackdown rises spectacularly to the south.

Descend through the fortified encampment, pass through the exit at the far side and continue down the hillside to a lane. Turn immediately to the left, in front of a cottage, and continue downhill to the valley bottom. The lane eventually reaches a gateway where it becomes a muddy track. Follow this track for a few hundred yards until a fence slopes down the hill on the right-hand side. Follow the muddy track alongside this fence, up the hillside, until you emerge onto a lane. Turn left, and you soon reach St Michael's church in Rowberrow, with its fine Perpendicular tower and normally locked door. Continuing along the lane, it is just a few hundred yards to the Swan.

Butcombe
The Mill Inn

Butcombe, an unspoilt little village, lies in the folds of the gentle hills to the north of Blagdon Lake. Real ale buffs around the country will be familiar with the name of Butcombe, for the village is home to an independent brewer that produces the fine Butcombe Avon Bitter. How appropriate, therefore, to find a genuine village local that has no frills or fancies and is quite simply a down-to-earth alehouse. The Mill Inn, a mixture of local stone and brickwork, sits at a road junction where a lane leads off to Nempnett Thrubwell – a delightful name, surely only to be found in what was rural Somerset.

The Mill Inn offers patrons a public bar, alongside which lies a small lounge. The bars are very traditional, with no signs of renovation or modernisation, simply a delightful hotch-potch of old-fashioned tables and chairs, the occasional wooden pew, plus window and alcove seats. Stone fireplaces provide welcome warmth during the winter months, with a fine pair of livestock horns gracing the wall above the fireplace in the public bar. Around the walls hang a number of large colour photographs, again with rural themes. There is one fine view of the Mill Inn, with another print showing a dog that has proudly rounded up a herd of cattle. There is no excuse for boredom at the Mill. Traditional pub games are available for patrons. Both bars have excellent table skittle sets as a definite attraction, conveniently placed on cast-iron treadle sewing machine bases. Of course, being a fine, unspoiled local, pride of place in the public bar is given to a piano.

The Mill Inn is very much a drinkers' pub, so do not expect haute cuisine. The only thing that can be guaranteed for lunchtime visitors is that massive cheese or ham rolls will certainly be available. Other than that, it will have to be those faithful pub standbys, such as pork scratchings, pickled eggs, peanuts and crisps. The beers, ales and ciders on offer are ample compensation, however. Naturally, Butcombe Bitter should be every visitor's first tipple. Other choices might include Oakhill or Simonds Bitter, Thatchers or a locally produced West Country cider.

This excellent village pub will certainly remind older visitors of the pubs of their youth.

Telephone: 0761 462406.

How to get there: Make for Blagdon, on the A368 Bath to Weston road. From the village, follow the unclassified road northwards that heads across the dam at the western end of Blagdon Lake. Butcombe lies a mile or so beyond the lake. You will easily spot the Mill Inn, located in the centre of this small village.

Parking: There is a car park for patrons, opposite the Mill Inn. There is also limited room for roadside parking in the vicinity of the inn.

Length of the walk: 2½ miles. Map: OS Landranger 172 Bristol and Bath (GR 514614).

Blagdon Lake and the neighbouring Chew Valley Lake supply much of Bristol's water requirements. Blagdon is an ornithologist's dream, with its wildfowl best described in Ken Hall's Where to Watch Birds in Somerset and Avon *(Helm). Blagdon's 550 acres and 1,700 million gallon capacity are both impressive statistics. Rolling hills lie to the north of Blagdon, with the small village of Butcombe nestling in one of the folds above the lakeside. As well as exploring the delightful landscape, this excellent short circuit brings fine views to the south across the Chew Valley to the imposing Mendip Hills beyond.*

The Walk
Follow the lane directly opposite the Mill Inn, leading to Nempnett. In 200 yards, at a T-junction, turn right and continue past Sage's Farm and on to Brook Farm. Just past the driveway to Brook Farm, cross the four-bar wooden stile on the right-hand side, into the corner of the

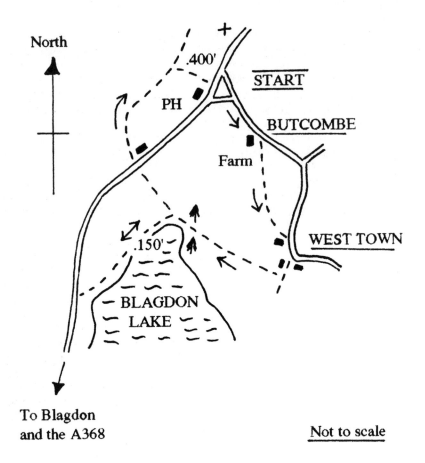

North

.400'

PH

START

BUTCOMBE

Farm

.150'

WEST TOWN

― BLAGDON
― LAKE ―

To Blagdon
and the A368

Not to scale

field. Follow the right-hand hedgerow to another stile in the far right-hand corner of this field, and cross into the next field. Cross the next field to the gateway opposite, a procedure that is repeated in the following field. Beyond this gateway, follow the left-hand hedgerow to another gate in the corner of the field, beyond which a track is followed to the left of a cottage and out on to a quiet country lane.

Turn right, follow this lane down to Bellevue Farm, and carry on down the lane ahead (signposted 'No Through Road To Lake'). Just past the cottage on the right-hand side, cross the stone slab stile on the right and go over the field ahead, to the clearly visible stile opposite. The views to the south are impressive, encompassing Blagdon Lake, the hillside village of Ubley and the Mendip Hills. Follow the right-hand field boundaries across the next three fields. In the far corner of the third field, a stile brings you into an area of carefully managed

114

woodland that borders the northern fringes of Blagdon Lake.

Follow the obvious path through the woodland – where deliberate clearing of conifers has removed much of the tree-cover – to a footbridge across one of Blagdon's feeder streams. In the next field, follow the left-hand field boundary to a stile and another footbridge. An almost obligatory detour is now in order. Cross the stile on the left-hand side, and follow the path that leads down to Blagdon Lake. How far you care to follow this path is your decision – perhaps just as far as the first view of the lake – but it is your only opportunity to get to the actual lakeside. At some point, retrace your steps back to the footbridge, and turn left to cross a stile into the adjoining field. Cross to a gap in the top right-hand corner of this field, beyond which you follow the left-hand hedgerow up to a gateway and the Blagdon to Butcombe road.

Follow the bridlepath opposite and climb past a couple of cottages and on up to the hilltop. The path, Sutton Lane, bears to the right, and follows the edge of the hilltop northwards. In a short distance, beneath a fine beech tree, the hedgerows that have blocked the view across Blagdon Lake disappear and a fine vista opens up. Continue along Sutton Lane for another 300 yards or so, to the second gateway on the right, just past a point where two sets of telegraph wires cross the bridlepath. Cross this gate, and follow the left-hand hedgerow downhill towards Butcombe. Cross the gate in the corner of the field, and follow the hedgerow on the right, downhill. At the foot of the hill, cross a footbridge over a small stream. Follow the right-hand edge of the field beyond this bridge out onto the lane in Butcombe, negotiating two or three stiles en route. Turn right at the road, and the Mill Inn is just a few yards down the lane.

Chew Magna was described in the 16th century as a 'pretty clothing town', by John Leland, Henry VIII's antiquary. The grand houses built above the raised pavements along the High Street certainly testify to the wealth that the cloth trade must have generated. At the eastern end of the village, opposite St Andrew's church, lies the Pelican inn. This whitewashed hostelry is now part of the Ushers empire, the West Country brewery based in Trowbridge. The inn fronts on to Chew's High Street and is a picture in summer months with its tubs and hanging baskets full of attractive floral displays. Inside the Pelican patrons will find a public bar and a lounge bar. Both are comfortably furnished and welcoming, with exposed stonework, wooden wall panelling and black beams, creating a traditional atmosphere. There is, of course, a fine stone fireplace, whilst around the walls hang a variety of rustic prints. The feature that will catch the eye of most visitors, however, is the bar itself. This is the only pub that I know of where a thatched roof decorates the bar, and an attractive feature it makes, too. The bunches of hops that hang from the thatch form an ideal complementary feature. Behind the inn is a small courtyard area that leads into a secluded walled garden, ideal for warm days.

The Pelican serves a good range of conventional pub food that is both well prepared and presented. The menu offers options such as toasted sandwiches, salads, jacket potatoes, ploughman's, steak and kidney pie, lasagne, fish dishes, sandwiches and soup. The toasted sandwiches have a number of appetising fillings, including bacon, cheese and tomato, whilst the jacket potatoes could be filled with either chilli, beans or tuna. Salad, chips or rice are always available to accompany your meal, too. Fine Ushers beers, such as Founders, Best Bitter and Triple Crown, are available at the Pelican, as well as Courage Bitter. As we are in what was north Somerset, a cider, such as Strongbow, may be more appropriate.

This is a refreshing pub in more ways than one. The character of Chew Magna has changed much in recent years, as it has developed into an upmarket commuter village, and many local youngsters can only dream of ever living in their home village. Despite the changes, the Pelican has remained as a solid, time-honoured local pub. Long may this continue!

Telephone: 0275 332448.

How to get there: Chew Magna lies south of Bristol on the B3130, the road that links the A37 at Pensford with the A38 at Barrow Gurney. The Pelican enjoys a prominent location at the eastern end of the High Street, fronting on to the main road.

Parking: There is a signposted public car park behind the Pelican. Alternatively, there is a limited amount of roadside parking outside the pub itself.

Length of the walk: 4½ miles. Map: OS Landranger 172 Bristol and Bath (GR 576632).

Chew Magna lies just to the north of the vast Chew Valley Lake, which supplies a high proportion of Bristol's water requirements. The walk explores the undulating countryside to the south of the village, before climbing Knowle Hill. This lofty vantage point brings views across the vast reservoir to the Mendip Hills beyond. From Knowle Hill, our steps descend to the lake, where a short stroll along a section of its northern shoreline will have twitchers positively twitching with excitement! From the reservoir, the walk returns to Chew Magna along the banks of the river Chew. It was the damming of this diminutive river in the 1950s that created the man-made lake with its capacity of 4,500 million gallons.

The Walk
Opposite the Pelican, follow the footpath that leads to St Andrew's church. The path bears to the right in front of the church, before forking. Take the right-hand fork, which runs alongside a high wall, before crossing a stile to join a gravelled driveway. Continue along this driveway as it passes Chew Court, the Coach House and the local cricket club, before joining the B3130.

Cross the road, and take the enclosed footpath opposite, down to the river Chew. Cross the river, and follow the path ahead as it borders the river for a short distance, before climbing a bank up into an open field. Head directly across this field to a stile in the opposite hedgerow, about 100 yards to the right of the river and just 10 yards to the right of a water trough. Continue across the middle of the next field, following a path that eventually drops down to a stone slab bridge where you recross the Chew. Turn right along the prominent track on the other side of the river and, in a short distance, where this track bears to the left, cross the gate directly ahead to enter an open field.

Aim for the gate/stile on the opposite side of this field, beyond which you should follow the bottom edge of the next three fields. The farmland hereabouts is lush meadow, with a marshy, wooded area to your right. At the far side of the third field, a diversion from the route shown on the OS sheets has taken place. The path no longer passes through the gardens of Moorledge, instead it bears to the left to follow the perimeter fence of this fine property. Where this fence ends, continue the short distance across the field to a gateway and a quiet country lane.

118

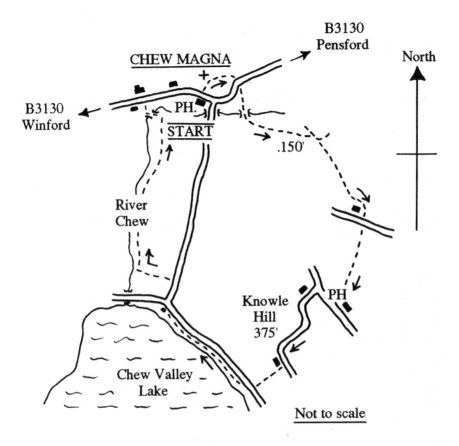

Across the road is another gateway. Cross to the opposite corner of the next field, walking in the direction of the whitewashed pub on the skyline. In the corner of this field, a couple of concrete pillars enable you to cross a small stream, beyond which you follow the left-hand field boundary to a stile. In the next field, climb up to the top corner, where a stile brings you out on the Chew Magna road, alongside the Pony and Trap pub – a convenient watering hole halfway around the circuit.

Turn right at the road and, in a short distance, left on to a lane signposted 'Knowle Hill'. This lane soon bears left and flanks the south-eastern slopes of the hillside before running around to the much modernised Knowle Hill Farm. Knowle Hill itself is common land, and I will leave you to work out a detour to the hilltop to obtain a quite superb view of the Chew valley.

Just past the farmhouse, cross a cattle grid on the right and walk

119

through to what was once the farmyard. It is now the driveway leading to a converted barn. The right of way passes to the left of the residence ahead, crosses a gate on the left-hand side and then bears right to follow the right-hand field boundaries, downhill to the Bishop Sutton to Chew Stoke road. Turn right at the road for a few yards, before turning left into a picnic area that borders Chew Valley Lake. Turn right at the lakeside to follow the right of way, going along the water's edge through to the next picnic site, ½ mile distant. This stroll along the edge of the reservoir is quite superb, with Chew Valley Lake holding internationally significant numbers of some wildfowl.

Leave this second picnic area via its official road exit, and follow a lane opposite signposted 'Denny Lane'. In just 150 yards, turn left to follow a Water Board access road that leads down to the reservoir's dam. In 300 yards, just before this road crosses the river Chew, turn right on to a signposted footpath. This well-defined path passes through a small area of woodland before entering open fields. Follow the footpath across the next six fields, back to Chew Magna. The path borders the river Chew to a greater or lesser extent, and is easy to follow, due to the large number of prominent stiles and waymarks.

In the final field, cross a stile in the left-hand corner, follow the path ahead to a lane and turn left. Continue along this path to a second bridge, beyond which you turn immediately to the right and follow a path up to Chew Magna High Street. Turn right, and walk past the village's fine houses back to the Pelican.

29 Dundry
The Dundry Inn

The sprawling suburbs of south Bristol end abruptly at the foot of Dundry Hill. High on the hilltop, at over 750 ft above sea level, stands the village of Dundry, overlooking one of England's great cities. S.P.B. Mais described the view from the village church as being 'one of the widest in all Somerset [with] all Bristol standing immediately below'. In the shadow of the splendid pinnacled tower of St Michael's stands the Dundry Inn, with its whitewashed walls and inn sign depicting the nearby church.

The Dundry Inn is a Courage house, with purple woodwork and turquoise wallpaper that may not be every visitor's favourite colour scheme – there is a small amount of exposed stonework, however, to satisfy the traditionalist. Around the walls hang a mixture of modern and antique prints, together with a collection of complementary copper items, such as bed-warmers and jugs. A number of cosy lounge areas are grouped around the central bar, with the main lounge containing a welcoming open fire in winter. The décor is completed by a number of dark-wood tables and chairs, together with some comfortable window seats.

An extensive bar menu is offered, drawing in customers from a wide

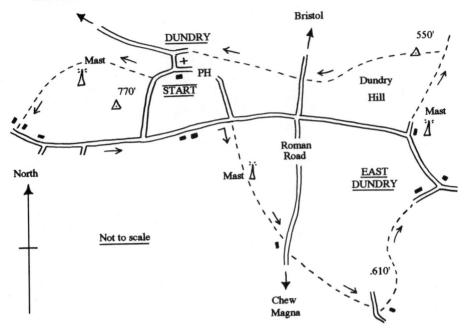

To Barrow Gurney
and the A38

DUNDRY

Bristol

550'

Mast

PH

Dundry
Hill

770'

START

Mast

North

Roman
Road

Mast

EAST
DUNDRY

Not to scale

.610'

Chew
Magna

area. Starters might include garlic mushrooms in mayonnaise or a North Sea prawn cocktail, whilst main courses are grouped under headings such as Dundry skins, Dundry oggys, French stick sandwiches, specialities, seafood dishes, platters and grills. The Dundry skins are fried potato skins with a choice of dips, such as Stilton and port, whilst the oggys are filled puff-pastry cases. Trawlerman's oggy, for example, contains a fresh fish filling. There is an equally extensive range of sweets, including Dutch apple tart and sticky toffee pudding with cream as well as custard. As this is a Courage house, it is not surprising to find Courage Bitter, Best Bitter and Directors available, whilst a typical guest beer might be Smiles Best Bitter, brewed by a local Bristol brewer.

Telephone: 0272 641722.

How to get there: St Michael's church, high on Dundry Hill, is visible from all over Bristol. To reach this lofty landmark, follow the A38 to the south-west of the city for 5 miles, before turning left on an unclassified road leading to Dundry. The Dundry Inn lies in the centre of the village, opposite the church.

122

Parking: The Dundry Inn has its own car park. Considerate walkers, however, would be better advised to use the village car park. This is signposted and lies just a short distance to the west of the inn.

Length of the walk: 6 miles. Map: OS Landranger 172 Bristol and Bath (GR 557669).

Motorists driving through the sprawling suburbs of south Bristol will often have looked beyond the tower blocks to the green hills beyond. This area of upland is Dundry Hill, with the village church in Dundry itself a notable landmark on the hilltop. This walk takes the visitor on to these hills, from where the views back across the city of Bristol are quite superb: deep rural countryside above the edge of creeping suburbia.

The Walk

Alongside the village car park, a gate leads into an open field. Follow the path beyond this gateway, across Dundry Down, as far as the second TV mast. To the right of this mast, in the corner of the field, is a stone slab stile. Cross the stile and head downhill towards Castle Farm. The views from this hillside are quite impressive, with the Barrow Reservoirs in the valley below sure to catch your eye. The official right of way runs through the farmyard but, unless you enjoy wading through ankle-deep manure, it is best to follow the short diversion recommended by the farmer! As you head down across the field, bear left to a gateway a short distance up from the farm itself. This gateway brings you out on the lane leading down to the farm. Turn left and follow this lane, uphill, for ¼ mile to the Winford to Dundry road. Turn left, and follow this quiet road for over ½ mile, past a small housing development on your right, and as far as a road junction with a left turn, signposted to Dundry.

At this junction you will find a stone stile on your right-hand side. Follow the left-hand field boundary beyond the stile as far as another mast. Cross the stile to the right of this mast, clip the corner of the next field to reach a second stile, and follow the left-hand field boundary beyond, as far as a pair of houses alongside the Chew Magna road. This section of the walk brings impressive views to the south across the Chew Valley Lake and the Mendip Hills beyond.

Turn right for just a few yards, before passing through the gateway on the left-hand side. Beyond this gate, follow the left-hand field boundaries through four fields to a quiet country lane. Turn right at the lane and in 100 yards, at a sharp bend, cross the stile on your left-hand side. The views continue to impress, only this time they are eastwards towards Maes Knoll.

Follow the right-hand field boundaries through the next two fields, until the path drops down into a shady dip, where the ground is damp underfoot due to a spring. In this dip is a gateway. Follow the damp, muddy path beyond the gate through to East Dundry, where it eventually becomes a metalled lane that leads up to the Dundry road. Turn left, and follow this road uphill to a junction alongside a farm. Continue along the bridlepath opposite, alongside North Hill Farm, to yet another mast. The bridlepath soon reaches open fields. Follow the right-hand field boundary downhill, through a couple of fields.

Turn left and go along the bottom hedgerow of the second field. If you search hard in the undergrowth on your right, you might discover a trig point (165 m on the OS sheets). This field path leads to a bridlepath, which eventually joins the Chew Magna to Bristol road, an old Roman thoroughfare. Cross over into Oxleaze Lane, which is followed for 150 yards to a road junction. Opposite is a wooden gate. Follow the bridlepath beyond this gateway back into Dundry, using the church tower as a landmark. To your right, the whole of Bristol is laid out at your feet. The path passes just below a farm before returning to the village.

Clevedon
The Campbell's Landing

Generations of holidaymakers visiting the Bristol Channel resorts of Clevedon, Weston-super-Mare and Ilfracombe will have enjoyed a trip on one of the old Campbell's paddle-steamers. Sadly, a cruise on the Channel is now but a memory. Opposite the entrance to Clevedon Pier, however, the Campbell's Landing attempts to recreate the atmosphere of one of the old steamers. The bar and restaurant are decorated with various items of Campbell's memorabilia – old timetables, publicity leaflets, historic photographs and a ship's figurehead. Even the toilets have a nautical feel, with their porthole windows and signs reading 'buoys' and 'gulls'. Reproduction tables and chairs fill the bar and restaurant, where patrons fortunate enough to find a window seat will enjoy views of the Channel itself.

The bar food consists of staple dishes such as soups, jacket potatoes and sandwiches, but there is a varied restaurant menu in addition. This is divided into a number of interesting categories – traditional/original starters, vegetarian/low calorie, Italiano, for fishmongers, for serious hunger, hot off the grill and simply terrific. A starter could be deep-fried cream cheese and Cumberland dip, a vegetarian dish,

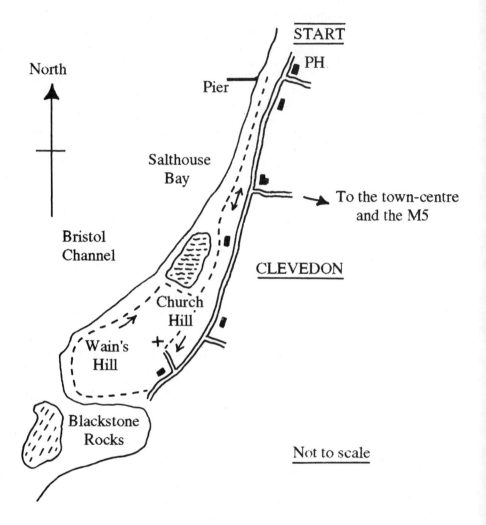

START

PH

North

Pier

Salthouse
Bay

To the town-centre
and the M5

Bristol
Channel

CLEVEDON

Church
Hill

Wain's
Hill

Blackstone
Rocks

Not to scale

parcels of stir-fried vegetables with ginger and, for serious hunger, a steak and kidney pie in stout. Perhaps even more impressive is a 'simply terrific' dish – rump steak smothered in fresh peppercorns, pan-fried and flamed in brandy.

Campbell's Landing is a freehouse, with a range of beers and ales to match. These might typically include Ruddles, John Smith's, Courage Bitter and Beamish Stout. There is also an extensive wine list, where, alongside the sparkling, red, white and rosé selections, sit a number of interesting house wines – Campbell's Landing red, dry white and medium dry white.

Telephone: 0275 872094.

How to get there: Clevedon lies alongside junction 20 of the M5 motorway, to the south-west of Bristol. Follow the signs to the sea front, where the Campbell's Landing will be found opposite the entrance to the pier.

Parking: There is roadside parking on the sea front, alongside Clevedon Pier. If this is full, park on one of the side roads in the vicinity.

Length of the walk: 2 ½ miles. Map: OS Landranger 172 Bristol and Bath (GR 403718).

Clevedon is a traditional Victorian coastal resort on the Bristol Channel, best known for its pier that earned the praises of Sir John Betjeman, no less. This short, easy walk explores the resort's promenade before climbing onto Church Hill and Wain's Hill. This small upland area forms a headland to the south-west of the town, bringing delightful views across the Channel to the Welsh coast. The walk around the headland is known as 'Poets' Walk' on account of the town's associations with the poet Coleridge. He had a cottage in nearby Old Church Road, from where he made frequent excursions around the local coast.

The Walk

From Clevedon's magnificent Victorian pier, walk along the promenade, passing the sailing club, the bandstand, the Little Harp Inn and the somewhat neglected open-air pool. At the end of the pool, the tarmac path ends. Climb the steps ahead to the summit of Church Hill, ignoring any side turns. The views from the top are quite superb, encompassing the nearby town, the hills south of Bristol and the Bristol Channel.

Continue across the hilltop, before following the footpaths down to St Andrew's church with its Norman tower. Follow the lane outside the church down to the road and turn right. This cul-de-sac borders the cemetery before ending at a wooden barrier. Beyond the barrier lies a small boatyard.

Just beyond this barrier, take the footpath on the right-hand side, which climbs to the western tip of Wain's Hill. A conveniently placed seat affords excellent views across the mud flats towards Weston-super-Mare. Continue around the headland, following the tarmac path, which eventually returns to the open-air pool. Retrace your steps along the promenade. The pier was only reopened to the public in 1989, following its collapse some 20 years earlier. Money is still neeed to complete the restoration of this magnificent Victorian monument – don't begrudge the toll!